STRATEGY IN VUCA TIMES

DON'T QUIT ON STRATEGY, YOUR BUSINESS STILL NEEDS IT

A GUIDE WITH KEY CONCEPTS AND EXPERIENCES TO MAKE YOUR BUSINESS THRIVE AMID PERMANENT CHANGE

JM PIQUÉ

STRATEGY IN VUCA TIMES

HOW YOUR BUSINESS CAN THRIVE AMID PERMANENT CHANGE

JM Piqué

About the author:

JM Piqué is an entrepreneur, consultant, and executive coach. Founder and Managing director at The Human Business - Management Consulting. Associate Professor at the Department of Strategy, Leadership and People at EADA Business School Barcelona, teaching Economy and Geopolitics, Strategy, and Change Management, Innovation, and Digital Transformation. He's been working for 25 years in research, management, and consultancy in public and private environments at an international level.

Table of contents

Introduction

Chapter 1
DON'T QUIT ON STRATEGY, YOUR BUSINESS STILL NEEDS IT

1. We Need to Define a New Corporate Strategy. Now
2. The Key To Master Strategy: Get Rid of Reality
3. Embrace Uncertainty, You Won't Be Safe Anymore
4. Many Businesses Still Live In The 1970s
5. Should Companies Do Politics?
6. Work for the Best, Be Ready for the Worst
7. Should Steve Jobs or Elon Musk Be a Role Model for Entrepreneurs?
8. Fears You'll Go Through In Your Entrepreneurial Journey, And How To Overcome Them

Chapter 2
GO BACK TO BASICS: A FEW SIMPLE CONCEPTS, BUT PERFECTLY IMPLEMENTED

9. How To Improve Strategy: Drucker Will Make Your Day
10. Don't Be a "Selfie Strategist"
11. The Need, The Product, And The Profit. As Simple As This

12. Focus On Actions, Not Words
13. Key Success Factors Every Business Should Think About
14. Why Business Fail? Is Your Company Making Lethal Mistakes?
15. Entrepreneurs Struggle To Come Back Stronger
16. Make Your Life Richer: Never Settle With First Impressions
17. Time For Turnaround Management: A True Story
18. Successful Entrepreneurs? Experience Is The Safest Way
19. When Being Authentic Can Make You Successful
20. Will You Take Care Of Your Relationships For A Longer And Happier Life?

Chapter 3
YOU CAN'T DO IT ON YOUR OWN: TEAM UP!

21. Cooperation Is Always The Best Option, In Business And Life
22. Do The Magic To Be In A Great Team
23. Unmasking The Fake Entrepreneur
24. The Power of Being Normal
25. How To Choose The Best Investor For Your Company
26. Forget About Quantity, Good Networking Is Based On Quality
27. How To Build Honest And Powerful Feedback
28. Build the Connectome of Your Business
29. How To Build Long Term Value: Successful Mentorships
30. Something's Changing On How Companies Deal With Employees

31. You Will Never Come Back To The Office, And This Is A Really Smart Move
32. The Basics of a High Quality Networking
33. Fear Is The Worst Enemy For Teams

CONCLUSION: Take control, you're in the driving seat

Introduction

Introductions are one of my favorite parts of any book because it is usually where the author gives you the context, the key motivations, how you should approach and read the book. Introductions are always very personal. Let me share a secret: many times, it's where I decide whether I'd read the book or not, and the part that sets the mood for the rest of the time writer and reader will be together.

That's why I'd like to share with you what's my view of this book. I think I wouldn't read it from the beginning to the end. I don't usually do that. These days, it's getting more challenging to finish a book, and we know it. The number of new pieces of information coming to us every minute, every second, may become literally unhealthy. Our diet has become a collection of finger food, leaving for exceptional moments a whole sequence of starters, main course, dessert, and maybe even a long conversation over coffee and the drinks of your preference, shared with loved ones and friends.

So, don't feel bad if you prefer reading this article, or the other, or just a couple of different ones. Go back and forth, leave it for a while, come back when something else rings a bell, and you recall that you saw something similar here. Our brains work like that these days.

Or, on the contrary, sit and read everything you want, all the articles back-to-back. It doesn't matter; the book is here to serve you, like a puzzle, to have a relaxed hour away, stop and have some thoughts, or compulsively look for some answers. Again, don't worry, it's not literature; it's much more like ideas and knowledge.

What I'd like to stress is the intention of the book. It's not an academic text backed with tons of research. Of course, we're talking about many things supported by science, but above all, this is built out of a collection of experiences, lessons, sometimes learned the hard way, through more than twenty-five years. I wouldn't ever write a memoir; let's put that in the first place. But I'm happy to share some a-ha moments, some things that annoyed me, the kind of things that seem to be so evident that you don't understand how it took so long to see they were screaming just in front of you. It's not advice, please, I'm nobody to say to anybody, "I've been there, don't make that mistake." You'll make own your own ones. I don't pretend to move the needle; you'll do that for you.

Main idea: strategy is not dead, but more powerful and needed than ever to get your business into the successful path, at least, into the alive path. That'd be the motto.

So, don't take this too seriously. It's just entertainment with some excellent ideas and tips to make you a better entrepreneur, C-level, or simply to be a better CEO of your life. Yes, you're your CEO. How are you planning to run your own life? If you think you don't need to have a part of you acting like your CEO, that's perfectly fine. It's just a technique.

But if you think it's worth doing some work organizing how to make your preferred future happen, keep reading; you'll find some exciting ideas.

I hope you enjoy it.

JM Piqué
December 2020

Chapter 1
DON'T QUIT ON STRATEGY, YOUR BUSINESS STILL NEEDS IT

Many have quit on strategy, as they think the world is changing so quickly that there's no point in planning anything. Go with the flow—surf the wave. Stay alive, and all the rest will come.

I think they're wrong. It's ok to keep driving forward, but at some point, you'd rather know where to go. Or maybe take it from another perspective: your clients like it when they see you have a purpose, clear goals, a direction, values, and principles, whichever they are. And they usually tend to reward that with some loyalty, even though it is only for a while.

It's always good to bear in mind key concepts and rules of thumb coming from experience. Some of them are not in the books, but they've been basically the same for ages. In this sense, don't get distracted by the fireworks of technology. Maybe everything is changing, but in many ways, the essential things are only taking new shapes but remaining the same in essence.

Chapter 1
DON'T QUIT ON STRATEGY, YOUR BUSINESS STILL NEEDS IT

1. We Need to Define a New Corporate Strategy. Now

Ten tips for a swoosh-shaped recovery that will make companies work hard on adjusting the corporate strategy

All being well, exit strategies are already on the go. If we can leave home in a month, start traveling in two, and in three months we learned how to take control of the situation through everyone's action and responsibility, going back to some normal will be a reality.

Pundits say that if public health response is active, and the interventions are somehow successful, recovery will develop slowly. China and the USA might come back to pre-crisis levels by the end of 2020 and Eurozone at the beginning of next year, depending on the depth and length of disruption, and the shape of recovery, which seems to point at a <u>swoosh-shape</u>.

Some trends will be just temporary and will recede with recovery, but others may last in our New Normal. According to many voices, the distance will remain higher, and concepts the Low-Touch or Contact-Free economy will be here to stay. The government will play a more critical role in the coordination of response to these new risks, a business will be subject to a higher degree of scrutiny, and some issues will come back to be top priorities, like environment, health, and privacy.

According to also to some initial analysis, demand and consumption will recover fast in a context of a constant flow of free money and next-to-zero inflation (at least for a year). Unfortunately, forecasts about employment are no that positive, and it may take a year to get over the situation.

Businesses will face troubled months ahead and will have to think quite a bit about strategic choices and priorities. Board of Innovation created a <u>quick matrix to help the decision-making process</u>: if you are in a business with a big impact and an L or U-shaped recovery perspective, you should give up and start something new as soon as you can. If your sector did not suffer severe damage, but the recovery will be slow (U-shaped), you should implement a defensive strategy to protect your advantage and search for new growth. But general guidelines are not enough, so we need to get a bit more into detail, so to be able to initiate action and be ready whenever the engine begins to work again.

In a recent webinar, we highlighted some of the aspects that companies should take into account to have a diagnosis, adjust priorities, and take action ASAP. The following are the ones we consider must be prioritized.

Survival: People, brand, and communication.

A company is nothing without its people, who will make a difference between getting past the crisis and thrive in the new context, or struggling in a long agony. People should be our first focus, their well-being, their conditions, their concerns, their personal and professional situation. We need to communicate with them fluently, transparently, timely, truly. And we need to build around a strong brand, a genuine one because the actions we take during the crisis are going to shape the bond and loyalty we're going to have with our clients and stakeholders. It's easy to fall onto passing an aggressive marketing campaign to balance the losses we're having. But what our consumers will think of us if our only concern is selling one more X while people are experiencing one of the most difficult personal and professional situations of their lives?

Check the basics of your strategy.

We need a mission, a vision, some strategic objectives, purpose, principles and values, competitive advantage, SWOT, value proposition, business model. It's an excellent opportunity to stop for a bit and confirm that everything's ok, or maybe we can adjust something to better deal with the situation and its consequences.

Get ready for the next crisis (don't have any doubt, it will come), and be ready for the comeback.

If you would have known this crisis was arriving, what would you have done? And of course, the pandemics can throw a new wave any time soon. Are our clients going to change their behavior in the future? Is our value chain going to be altered in some way? Imagine tomorrow you can come back to work at full steam, what would you need to be completely ready? WE don't expect a V-Shaped, but time flies, don't let the recovery catch you off guard.

First things first: take care of your financials

Have a close look at the numbers. How much time do you have before getting into serious trouble? Do you need any help? Are there any tools you could use as a resource to navigate the crisis? Make the worst-case scenario. Will you be able to cope with it? How? Can you imagine how the budget of 2021 going to be? Draft it and check whether it makes sense.

Compliance, insurances, responsibilities

Do you know if you have insurance for this situation? Are your compliance matters neatly arranged? Safety at work plans are ready? If you need to let someone go, do you have a clear view of your responsibilities, actions, and duties? Many companies are dusting off these days many contracts they haven't touched for years, make sure everything's in place.

Stress management, anxiety, uncertainty

As normal as we want to behave, it's tough to focus on anything when your mind is wandering around, worried about health, loved ones, your whole future. Ask them if they're ok, offer them help, have a conversation about the situation, fears. Realize a little bit of the stress we're all going through. It'll be more than rewarding.

Create the Recovery Team

It is quite apparent. We need to share, and we need to know what kind of intel we need, what kind of action we should take. Share with the team. Collect ideas, look for solutions, name names, and make things happen. Create a sense of coping with the situation of dealing with it, of having quick wins. In a word: take control and let the world see you are behind the wheel.

Innovate. Change is needed

Another obvious one. Is your organization innovation-friendly? Are we finding much resistance against change? Are we all living in our comfort zone, and prefer to remain there? Would you be able to launch a new spin-off of your business before the end of the year?

Remote work, and in general, work organization

We were pushed, almost thrown, to remote work during the last few weeks. We did not have a plan, or the abilities, without the tools, without some rules. Ok, we're better than a month ago, but it shouldn't go this way. It's time to sit and plan a proper strategy. We're ready now, but the teams need guidance, and the organization needs objectives and a clear direction.

Create a community

Power up. With your clients, with your providers, with your stakeholders. Networks are the hierarchies of the 21st Century. Use them, enjoy them, and make the most of it.

We created this quick list after reading a lot, funneling much content, helping many companies to figure out which is their current situation and options, and putting our own experience to the service of an unprecedented situation.

We hope it will be of help. And of course, we are open to any constructive discussion to help businesses.

2. The Key To Master Strategy: Get Rid of Reality

To some extent, a strategy is more an art than a technique, but we can try to follow some simple steps to take it to our best.

"The best way to predict the future is to create it", Peter Drucker.

Compared to the future, the present is simple, as it has only one version: reality. Relax, this is not an article about quantum mechanics, Schrodinger's cat, or The Matrix; it's just about strategy, and we'll try to give you some tips and tricks to become a good strategist.

You'll find a thousand definitions of what strategy is. Still, it comes down to the same concept: strategy is your plan to achieve an objective, to go from A (your situation today) to B (the condition in which you want to be). When you put it like this, it seems quite easy to grasp and produce, but we all have experienced the difficulty in defining a strategy and making it happen. Most of the time, it is, I'm sorry, our fault, because we leave the "strategy mode," get trapped in reality, and screw our ability to keep looking at the big picture, which is crucial for your strategic skills. Sometimes, people do not realize that they are in the opposite mindset to get a decent strategy production. And remember: it's impossible to be focused on the future and the present at the same time. Just like in a photograph: the more you approach your subject, the more challenging to keep foreground and background focused.

Maybe we should put an example related to our senses. When driving, you need to be strategic: look ahead, the cars around, the weather, the road signs, potential emerging and unexpected obstacles, thinking about the best alternative if you find a traffic jam. If you look attentively at your driving wheel, at the gear stick, you're dead. We clearly understand this, but sometimes we forget to look around, long, in our business, as it is easier to concentrate on your latest problem or the last quarter's P&L.

Therefore, reality kills strategy. Let's go step by step and try to maintain your strategic abilities and performance at its best, through a natural sequence that everyone can follow, just like your "strategic mantra." We know everyone knows that strategy is more an art than a technique, so we are trying to do something like the terrific, classic, <u>Friendship Algorithm</u> "created" by Sheldon Cooper. But anyway, we'll try.

How should you think about strategy?

First, let's agree on what we're talking about. Our definition for strategy would be "anticipating the future through the analysis of many options, and the action to make the preferred one happen." With strategy, what you do is maximizing the odds of your desired future and minimize the risks of reality to derail into any other option. It's important to understand that, with strategy, the only thing you do is try to increase the probability of the future to be close to your objective. You reduce uncertainty. And through this, we make clear that having no strategy means leaving the future to be random. This could be reasonable in times of extreme uncertainty or when we need to get into "survival mode," but even in very volatile situations, we have a capacity, to some extent, to influence the course of events to our interest. So from our perspective, it's always good not to leave our strategy to "random."

You have a third way. Many people use it. You can leave strategy to be random, and create a narrative to explain how you made "random reality" happen. It seems weird, and you have to be extremely talented in storytelling, but it's always an option that we could define as "anti-strategic" strategy. Go where the wind blows.

So, once we know we want to have an active strategy, let's go to the three steps to take control and be sure you're doing your best.

Put yourself into "Strategic Mode."

We already know we are biased by reality because we're living in it. After all, it touches us every minute, so we tend to think that reality is everything, and the only possible. But we know that to get the hang of strategy, we need to imagine a future taking into account many things, reality among them, but also potential trends, changes, behaviors, future events, forecasts, unexpected events, and everything at the same time—what a mess. We are so hardwired to the things we see that it's difficult to think about other alternatives.

What can we do? Our suggestion is to exercise. Play Go for an hour. Yes, the 25-century-year-old strategy <u>game</u>. Or play chess. Anything that forces you to see the big picture. Anything that forces you to take into account several variables at the same time, as well as their interaction, influence, and the possible consequences of every movement. The strategy is about thinking ten steps ahead and come back, doing the same many times for different options.

Another good exercise, which many people do as a productivity hack, but it is fundamentally a strategy game, is thinking of your actions in terms of getting at least two different results for every move. Do not do anything if it doesn't serve at least two different objectives. It boosts your impact, but besides, forces you to see consequences form many different perspectives, and get control of interdependences. So, to get into practice, think about the next thing you have on your agenda, and see how you can use it to have a "second result," besides the most obvious one.

The understand—inform—analyze sequence

You see a situation, you want to change it, and decide how future reality should look, according to your goal. So you identify the future you want to create, how you want to guide reality to that future. You understand some of the variables involved, but you don't have a clue about many others. That's why you need to get information about all of them and analyze all the knowledge you can gather according to your objective. There are many options to make your preferred future happen; you need to "walk" all the alternatives, see what you're going to find on your way, dismiss the ones that might lead to a dead-end, discard the riskiest, do some push to remove obstacles. You could draw a mental map, sketch some charts, think about it, take notes, have a conversation. Whatever works best for you. But you need to walk to the future and explore the best way before it comes.

To that, it is essential to get much information. Be a bit obsessive about retrieving, going over, as much knowledge as you can. The more you "eat," the fewer surprises you will encounter on your way to "your" future.

With all the information gathered, try to think about your strategy taking into account everything at the same time. It's time for analysis, options, influences, and side effects, synergies, unexpected discoveries, and hidden relations. Get in front of the big picture and try to find meaning. It might take time, a lot of back and forth, but this moment is paramount for your strategy.

We need to say that you can run the sequence both ways: from understanding to analyzing, or from analyzing to understanding. Some prefer to adapt reality to our objectives (I want to live on Mars, though now it seems impossible). Some others are more comfortable defining the goals with the foundation of reality (I want to act step by step against climate change, as I see it's worsening and becoming an emergency). There's no right or wrong; the only thing you need to check is that you want a specific future, and you have the tools to max the odds for it to happen.

And here it comes the art: now do the painting.

Coming back to Peter Drucker's quote at the beginning, we need to create our future. It doesn't exist, and we need to make it happen. You can try to guide and force creativity and innovation, but at some point, it will involve some lightbulb moments. We all know where, how we usually find the aha, when "all makes sense." We'll leave this to you, but we will insist that the moment is needed, catch it as soon as it comes, document it (it usually takes no more than half an hour to jot it down), sleep over it, and you'll develop later. Hard work is already done. Create something understandable that anyone can digest, and start working on the deployment and details.

As surprising as it may seem, in companies, we find more executors than strategists, even at C-level. That's why strategists find it so difficult to make the rest see the big picture. Though it may appear to be a matter of just a "click," it can be useful to provide everyone with tools to help develop a mindset that is not natural for a majority.

That was the only intention of this article, which would also like to stimulate reflection.

Don't let a stubborn reality ruin your bright future.

3. Embrace Uncertainty, You Won't Be Safe Anymore

In the twentieth century, being robust and permanent was a strength. Today, it is a hindrance and a burden.

You'll be safe and surrounded by certainties. This is what all of us seek, as a child who expects their parents will always have a solution when they cannot find a way out of a problem. We want to rely on a wild card, a magic formula that does not exist in this Age of Uncertainty, as defined by the economist John Kenneth Galbraith in 1977. Fortune is still present, as it always has been, to bring excitement to everything we do.

Much has been theorized and published about how capitalism is exhausted as a productive system. Or, at least, there's an ongoing profound transformation, caused, mainly, by the extraordinary advancement of information and telecommunications technologies in recent decades. The global scenario has dramatically changed due to the need to renew the energy model. More than twenty years ago, Peter Drucker already stated that we were facing a paradigm shift, in which "the basic economic resource, the means of production, is no longer capital, natural resources, or labor, but rather knowledge. Today, value is generated by productivity and innovation, which are applications of knowledge to work ". In 2000, Lester Thurow also said that "knowledge is the new basis of wealth. It had never been.

In the past, when capitalists spoke of their wealth, they referred to factories, equipment, and natural resources they owned. In the future, when capitalists talk about their wealth, they will mean the control they have over knowledge."

All this conceptual mess is indeed typical of historical moments when crisis reigns in all senses. Companies find themselves amid an economic, financial, environmental, and social earthquake, in which the number of uncertainties far exceeds that of certainties. However, businesses need to keep going; they must continue operating, changing, and surviving day by day. We wish we could stop the economy for a while to fix it, repair the damaged parts, and fine-tune the machine to face the new situation with guarantees. But this does not seem possible.

We should not forget that change is, actually, our natural state. Zachary Karabell recounted it a few years ago in his blog The Edgy Optimist: "We have reached a critical point in which the model that has been successful so far will not serve for the future. The agricultural society of the 19th century gave way to the industrial of the 20th century, giving way to the economy of services, ideas, and technology in the 21st century. None of those transitions has happened without pain and disruption, and the current transition will be no exception."

It is complicated to imagine people and organizations that can carry out all these changes without a fundamental element as an engine: motivation, a sense of the in-depth trends, and, ultimately, confidence in one's abilities in this context. Let's put it another way: happiness, the feeling of moving forward.

Perhaps that is one of the most significant learnings that we must face in our lives, as individuals and as entrepreneurs: that our decisions will be ours alone, and we will permanently bear the burden of responsibility and consequences. No one will share our mistakes, and everyone will want our successes.

Therefore, we must transform the personal and business mentality, corner the short term, or at least not grant it all the time and space. And at the same time, step by step, look a little further and develop a future project. Obstacles will come no matter what, and maybe something new can be built in the meantime.

4. Many Businesses Still Live In The 1970s

And that seems to be absolutely fine for many.

Let me ask you something: how outdated seems this next paragraph? How far and unfair, or how close and relevant sounds to you?

"The businessmen believe that they are defending free enterprise when they declaim that business is not concerned "merely" with profit but also with promoting desirable "social" ends; that business has a "social conscience" and takes seriously its responsibilities for providing employment, eliminating discrimination, avoiding pollution and whatever else may be the catchwords of the contemporary crop of reformers. In fact they are — or would be if they or any one else took them seriously — preaching pure and unadulterated socialism. Businessmen who talk this way are unwitting puppets of the intellectual forces that have been undermining the basis of a free society these past decades."

These were the words published by Milton Friedman in The New York Times, exactly 50 years ago, in September 1970. The famous article's title couldn't be more of a statement: "The Social Responsibility Of Business Is to Increase Its Profits." Period.
Unwitting. Puppets. Undermining. Free. Society. Is that clear enough? I'm not sure I'd have him as a boss.

Any CEO's responsibility is "to conduct the business in accordance with the shareholder's desires, which generally will be to make as much money as possible."

Beyond the fury that the text conveys, he probably gave voice to the opinion of many at that time. And unfortunately, in my view, this is the perspective of many, still today. As Binyamin Appelbaum points out in the New York Times, "for decades, policymakers have embraced his advice. They have slashed taxes, sought to undermine unions, and reduced some kinds of regulation, notably in financial markets. Regulators made it easier for companies to shovel money to shareholders," leading to "depressingly clear results. Growth has slowed, and much of the available gains have been pocketed by a small minority of very wealthy Americans. The shareholding class keeps getting richer; the rest of the nation is falling behind."

I think his point is quite right: instead of criticizing Friedman, what we should do if we disagree with his theories, is giving more power to a more conscious government.

Friedman wanted to unleash greed and give it all the room to grow to its highest. How would we do that? Shrinking the public sector to a shadow of what it used to be. Put a fence around your property, buy a gun, and shoot anyone wandering around. Don't ask.

Let's come back to the extreme version of freedom.

The question is that, for the business to focus on maximizing profit for shareholders, someone must be working on innovation. Yes, Mr. Friedman, people are working on increasing productivity to make it possible for you to keep surfing on greed.

At that time, in 1970, the USA government just landed on the moon. And during the 1960s, the Advanced Research Projects Agency Network (ARPANET) was the first wide-area packet-switching network with distributed control and one of the first networks to implement the TCP/IP protocol suite. Both technologies became the technical foundation of the Internet.

Fifty years later, the "trillion-dollar companies" reign in the market and make equivalent amounts of profit. Public investment from fifty years ago is making the world go round today.

So it's ok to be short-sighted and say that the only thing your business cares about is the highest possible profit, no matter what. But at least, they should admit that someone's working for them to keep having this profit. Do you want to turn a blind eye onto all the rest? Go ahead. But free-riders might not be welcome anymore.

Those 1970s ended up being the decade of a deep crisis, continued by Friedmanesque president like Ronald Reagan and supported by a wave of neoliberal economic policies. The end of manufacturing in the Ms. Thatcher's UK, and The Bonfire of the Vanities in the USA, led to the fall of the Berlin Wall, globalization, and the End of History. And so on.

What do we mean? The world has changed dramatically in the latest fifty years. Even the Business Roundtable announced in 2019 the release of a new Statement on the

Purpose of a Corporation signed by 181 CEOs, who commit to lead their companies for the benefit of all stakeholders — customers, employees, suppliers, communities, and shareholders.

Since 1978, Business Roundtable was inspired by Friedman's ideas, periodically issuing Principles of Corporate Governance that include language on a corporation's purpose. Each version of that document issued since 1997 stated that corporations exist principally to serve their shareholders.

But in 2019, they finally said that "each of our stakeholders is essential. We commit to deliver value to all of them, for the future success of our companies, our communities and our country." Signed by: Jeff Bezos, Tim Cook, Satya Nadella, among the most important businessmen in America (not many women around, by the way).

The shareholder was not anymore the one and only. What a pity.

The coin has flipped. At least, that's the official statement.

Though, it seems that stock market prices are still more important than employment. Or to put it another, more painful way, profit goes first, and lives would go after. Dan Patrick, Texas' Republican lieutenant governor, suggested during the coronavirus pandemic that he and other grandparents would be willing to risk their health and even lives in order for the United States to "get back to work." "Those of us who are 70 plus, we'll take care of ourselves. But don't sacrifice the country."

Indeed, many companies leaped to support the COVID-19 response. The key factors that enabled both large and small firms to be first movers were a willingness to innovate boldly and partner quickly based on established relationships with governments, non-profits, and other companies. For those companies, creativity and trusted networks enabled agility that benefited the public interest — and in many cases, it brought business benefits.

But still, many others are thriving amid the pandemic. Amazon added 400 billion to its market cap, and Microsoft and Apple more than 200. And the list is long: Tesla, Tencent, Facebook, Alphabet, Netflix, etc.

By the way. As he was promoting his new book, Netflix's CEO, Reed Hastings, said that "we are off to a faster start in growth than any year in our history, roughly from 160 million to 190 million. So, a lotta growth. COVID, unfortunately, is everywhere, and luckily Netflix is, too."

Netflix's shareholders must be very happy to hear their CEO say that.

5. Should Companies Do Politics?

Economic, social, and political circumstances have led to a new normal, and consumers now demand companies to openly and clearly show their views.

It's not supposed to be the companies' job. As a business, their priority is doing business. P&L is my only God, and I don't serve anything or anyone else. On the contrary, we know companies cannot be an island amidst all the context we're living. They have workers who are sensitive to many of the hot topics they see around. And they also have customers who want to buy products with which they can feel comfortable, aligned, and represented. No one wants to be ashamed of the things they buy. Most of us are willing to outsource our responsibility through buying things that contribute to sustainability, social justice, and living conditions.

We know that many companies have a CSR strategy to promote marketing, PR activities and gain reputation. We know that many companies get in trouble, and its market position is damaged by expressing their views and opinions, just because half of the world doesn't share that view.

The companies' question is that it's becoming impossible not to participate in the troubled world we're living in today. Whichever side are you (and being in no side is always read as one more choice, sometimes the worst of all.)

And we're not only talking about those companies which founders or principles show strong values or a commitment to certain aspects. We're not either talking about those who contribute with donations to candidates, expecting some kind of benefits or favours in the future.

Regarding the former, we have very well known examples, like Ben&Jerry's (in 1988, it was one of the first companies in the world to place a social mission in equal importance to its product and economic missions). Regarding the latter, we have also many examples (amid several scandals and public relations fiascos, Facebook spent $12,620,000 on lobbying in 2018.)

According to a recent research paper by the National Bureau of Economic Research, 57.7% of large-company CEOs consistently donated to Republicans, while only 18.6% donated to Democrats, with the rest leaning toward neither party.

First one's actions, the "idealist" type, don't need to be especially related to politics, a party, or a candidate; the second one's, the "lobbyists," are not usually related to principles but to profit.

In between the two, some express their political views in an apparent act of responsibility:

Rob Rhinehart, a co-founder of nutritional drink start-up Soylent, declared in a blog post last week that he was supporting Kanye West for president. "I am so sick of politics," Mr. Rhinehart wrote. "Politics are suddenly everywhere. I cannot avoid them."

David Barrett, the chief executive of Expensify, a business software start-up, went in another direction. In an email to his company's 10 million customers last week, he implored them to embrace politics by choosing the Democratic presidential nominee, Joseph R. Biden Jr. "Anything less than a vote for Biden is a vote against democracy," Mr. Barrett proclaimed.

For example, in Silicon Valley, tech workers have long been regarded as liberal but not politically overactive. But politics and social issues have become so omnipresent in every corner of reality that is almost impossible to keep away from it: "There's no real separation anymore, in the current political climate, between politics and everything else. It has permeated absolutely everything," said Bradley Tusk, a venture capitalist and political consultant.

However, these positions come usually at a high cost, as public opinion is not used or ready to understand this as a simple, legitimate, and sometimes even inevitable, manifestation of the person behind the CEO, or the expression of a company view from the perspective of its responsibility towards the environment in which it lives.

Mesut Özil, the soccer player, spoke out strongly on his Instagram account against China's persecution of the Uighur population in the north-western region of Xinjiang and criticized Muslims for not doing more to highlight the issue. The post got more than 800,000 likes, but on the contrary, his club, Arsenal, distanced themselves from comments. Wherever it began, this is where it has led: 10 months later, Mesut Özil has, effectively, been erased.

NBA players and #BlackLivesMatter have been in the news extensively. On a conference call with more than 80 players, Kyrie Irving said he didn't feel right playing professional basketball under the circumstances, and he believed that sports would only be a distraction from pursuing equality. Donald Trump said that "The NBA has become so political that nobody cares about it anymore. LeBron is a spokesman for the Democratic party and a very nasty spokesman."

Is it still possible for companies, in 2020, to pretend they don't see anything around them, just to avoid the negative effects of taking a side? Some psychologists keep saying that having a political stance is a bad idea, basically for two reasons: first, they say it usually alienates a significant fraction of the company's customers, employees, investors, and other constituents. And second, it takes the attention of managers away from the company's core business objectives.

But consumers are changing quickly, leaving not much room for companies to remain in a carefully neutral position. According to data from a Sprout Social survey of 1,000 consumers that may help, two-thirds of respondents said they wanted companies to take a stand on political issues, and 58 percent wanted them to do so on social media:

Brands face more reward than risk. Consumers' most common emotional reactions to brands taking a stand on social were positive, with intrigued, impressed and engaged emerging as the top three consumer reactions. Likewise, when consumers' personal beliefs align with what brands are saying, 28% will publicly praise a company. When individuals disagree with the brand's stance, 20% will publicly criticize a company.

It seems everything is aligning to push the companies to show something they usually kept for themselves or left to individuals' freedom and privacy.

As HBR explains, there was a time when companies, big and small, shied away from politics. But the state of the world today makes it almost impossible not to show up and speak your views. Some companies have already done it, and results are mixed but clear as Inc. showed with some examples like Gucci, Patagonia, or Nike.

The whole idea is that being passive is no longer enough. If you don't take action, it means you don't care. It is not enough to simply not be racist; now, it can be demanded to be actively anti-racist.

6. Work for the Best, Be Ready for the Worst

An interview with Lukas Yla, a Lithuanian entrepreneur.

We recorded the interview with Lukas in Vilnius, about a year ago, when he was already popular because of some of his achievements. Maybe you heard about him as **"the doughnuts guy"** whom they were talking about at Good Morning America, but he's already more than that. He's currently the **CEO of Citybee** and has been selected as one of the **Forbes 30 Under 30 in Technology**.

However, he describes himself as **"the regular guy, always competing with myself to be the best possible person in my professional and personal life."** He had a clear mind since he was very young: "many teenagers try to get attention by having the stupid haircut; I was amazed by the idea of building companies and business. Curiosity played a major role for me growing up."

It's challenging to find someone so decided and ready to be coherent and walk the talk. "I decided from a very young age that working should be fun. **Today I keep waking up with a smile and happily going to work**". "As a teen, I liked Adobe Photoshop, so I started going to contests with my friends, and I thought I could make money with that skill." Instead of competing against other kids, he grabbed a phonebook and started offering companies to develop their websites, copying the competition and the coolest pages from the USA. He crossed some lines and learned a lot from the real world. While studying Political Sciences at the university, he thought he had too much free time, so he started a new side project: buying books on Amazon and learning as much as he could about marketing.

He seems so confident saying that you only need to focus on what's under your control; the rest does not matter. And he believes so. There's always a way for him, and his friends keep telling him **he's like the one they can throw under the bus and stands up once and again as nothing happened**. 'As long as I'm alive, I keep going forward; I think it became a routine, a habit.' Adaptability is the key to him. He learned to deal with emotions when hard times come, just focusing on every possible solution, staying on the positive side. 'I keep getting prepared for the worst, and if it does not come, it feels quite easy. I never panicked, for me, it's like wasting a lot of time and energy, but now I think about it, I believe maybe I'm not going too fast, and I should push harder' says with a smile. 'When I have distress, I go to the gym and burn it. When you exercise, you realize discipline is so important'. In general, he wants to leave a healthy life.

The only moment when he's close to meltdown is when somebody doesn't meet the expectations. Though it may happen often, he keeps on the positive side, and try to do his best to help. **He is breaking the reality into pieces that everyone can choke—rationality to the max**.

He also shares some of his **productivity hacks, the best advice he received, life-changing books, and many other ideas**. He's an outstanding guy, and you should keep an eye on his movements because I'm sure you'll hear a lot about him in the future.

7. Should Steve Jobs or Elon Musk Be a Role Model for Entrepreneurs?

It seems like humility goes against all the traits that make a good entrepreneur. Could we change the cocky entrepreneur into a more caring one?

A question has been rounding my mind for years: what kind of entrepreneur should I be? Should I go for the alpha type "I-will-make-it-no-matter-what", "you-better-get-your-sh*t-done-before-I-get-mad"? On the contrary, should I be the balanced "I-have-a-life-beyond-this-project," "it-was-nice-but-maybe-it's-time-to-turn-the-page"?

This usually brings me to a second, more profound question. Do you need to be (or at least appears to be) a tough selfish jerk to be a successful entrepreneur? I know that developing your project, you'll encounter many insurmountable obstacles, and you'll need a faith beyond any limit. Carrying such a burden can turn you into a grumpy inflexible character sometimes. But is there any other way? Or we all need to be like in Startup or Succession TV shows?

My third and final related question would be: if you need to balance customer and grit, what should be the percentage for each? A friend was putting it funnily. Imagine you go to a girl and tell her: we're getting married tomorrow, I know I can be the love of your life, I have everything you want, and I'm sure you'll like me. The girl says, "wait, should I have a say on that?" and you go, "what? don't you see you have in front of you the best product you can get in the market?."

As an entrepreneur, I'm having trouble knowing when to push, when to stop, when it's time to wait or go full steam to sure death. And I think this is very much related to your character. I want to find a way to be strong without being cocky.

Tell me the truth: would you say Steve Jobs was a humble person? Although one of his most famous quotes was that "Stay Hungry, Stay Foolish," a thousand profiles of his personality do not especially depict humility. An interesting article about him written by Vishal Noel a few months ago mentioned a "customer obsession," highlighting that you need to "Get closer than ever to your customer. So close that you tell them what they need well before they realize it themselves."One of Job's principles was to "Become the storyteller-in-chief."

To me, that sounds a tad like, "you know nothing, let me do you a favor and sell you the solution to the need you don't even know you have, and I'm going to create."

Don't get me wrong. I admire a lot those who can be trailblazers, who are persistent enough when everybody thinks they are nuts—those whose faith in their product goes beyond any reason, setback, or disaster.

Those are the ones whom we can call proud. Of themselves, of what they are doing, of their ideas. They see no other option than success, though if we know their name, it's because they are part of the one percent who made it. The other ninety-nine percent we don't know was probably as proud and sure of their idea as the successful ones. Talking about Steve Jobs, <u>Business Insider</u> said: His mammoth personality could inspire those around him just as easily as it could tear them down:

When Apple was about to reveal the "Bondi Blue" iMac, he berated his good friend and ad partner Lee Clow over the phone. Jobs said Clow's team was getting the color wrong for the print ads. He shouted, "You guys don't know what you're doing. I'm going to get someone else to do the ads because this is fucked up."

We love to side with winners. They are so attractive; they are whom we'd secretly love to be; it's so difficult not to worship them.

Other names come quickly to our minds, and those usually come hand in hand with a word: obsession. To levels that most of us would consider an illness.

He has this unbelievable drive to work 70, 80, 90 hours a week, non-stop. There was a mattress on the floor in one bedroom, and about 30 Chinese food-to-go containers. That was it. He would sleep under his desk probably one in every three nights, sometimes one in two. Sleep wasn't his reward for hard work, sleep was the thing getting in the way.
He is the most relentless person I have ever met in my entire life.

Of course, they are talking about Elon Musk. It's not easy to live around a man like this, and especially living under him can be a nightmare.

'I've spent all my money and all of my friendships on this. It has to succeed. You need to do whatever is possible to make this happen—you need to use special forces methods to make this transmission happen.'

Coming back to Jobs, interviewing a job candidate from Isaacson's book:

"How old were you when you lost your virginity?" he asked. The candidate looked baffled. "What did you say?" "Are you a virgin?" Jobs asked. The candidate sat there flustered, so Jobs changed the subject. "How many times have you taken LSD?" Hertzfeld recalled, "The poor guy was turning varying shades of red, so I tried to change the subject and asked a straightforward technical question." But when the candidate droned on in his response, Jobs broke in. "Gobble, gobble, gobble, gobble," he said, cracking up Smith and Hertzfeld. "I guess I'm not the right guy," the poor man said as he got up to leave.

Philanthropist Ray Dalio, the billionaire investor and founder of Bridgewater Associates, asked some of the world's most successful entrepreneurs to take a one-hour personality test to identify their leadership qualities. Each businessman had similar results, at least, in one key category: some of the top leaders score low when it comes "concern for others."

Should we pursue this as a role model? Should we accept this as the price you need to pay to have a successful genius? This can be very closely intertwined with reality. Would it be naive to even dream of any other model?

When business schools train future leaders, they don't teach them to be the bully type. You learn how to pivot, listen to your customer, and create a diverse, engaged, happy team.

I'm not necessarily advocating for the perfect ideal entrepreneur, which would, of course, be great: "Entrepreneurs play a direct and active role in creating the building blocks of an ecosystem. This includes laying the foundations of an entrepreneurial culture, educating prospective entrepreneurs, providing skill training through innovative programs, and creating ecosystem infrastructure through industry organizations. They also bring up the next generation of entrepreneurs through informal schools of entrepreneurship often in parallel with developing their own ventures." Let's go towards this direction, but in the meantime, shall we simply create a "caring" entrepreneur?

Would it be then the idea of "Humble Entrepreneur" an oxymoron?

Harvard Business Review puts it very clear: "Passion is the fuel that entrepreneurs need to keep going. Research shows that Passion is a key predictor of entrepreneurs' creativity, persistence, and venture performance. In other words, the more passionate the entrepreneur, the more likely they are to succeed." And of course, the more Passion, the more demand, the more pressure, the more ego, the less patience.

It's like we're seeking here for a completely new breed. I need to admit I have not a clear example of the type. Do you know some? And besides, do you think it's possible?

8. Fears You'll Go Through In Your Entrepreneurial Journey, And How To Overcome Them

We put together some practical Q&A, talking about the many things entrepreneurs have in common.

Please raise your hand those entrepreneurs who did not think about giving up at least a handful of times, when not dozens. You know the saying: what's the top priority of an entrepreneur? Being alive tomorrow morning, to wake up and keep pushing.

Though most seem to be in a relentless pursuit for success (see our previous article), let's face that being an entrepreneur can be daunting. It might be psychologically only within reach of very few people. Did you ever hear an entrepreneur saying 'ok, I screwed up, it's time to go home'. Never. If you're a TRUE one, surrender cannot be part of your vocabulary. Surr... what?

But fear exists. All the time, no one is immune. Who says that? Many studies. We won't go through them, but those interested can have a look at good articles like The Unspoken Emotional Cost of Being an Entrepreneur, 5 Psychological Burdens of Being an Entrepreneur, There is a mental health crisis in entrepreneurship, here's how to tackle it, or Investors and entrepreneurs need to address the mental health crisis in startups.

Entrepreneurs could be considered to have superpowers. Or at least some of them.

So it's ok not to be ok. For some time. Don't you believe me?

Research has shown that start-up founders are:

- Twice as likely to suffer from depression.
- Six times more likely to suffer from ADHD.
- Three times more likely to suffer from substance abuse.
- 10 times more likely to suffer from bipolar disorder.
- Twice as likely to have a psychiatric hospitalisation.
- Twice as likely to have suicidal thoughts.

Let's assume that in a portfolio of 20 companies, 15 of them fail or underperform. That would mean that 10 of the 15 companies (65 percent) failed for avoidable "human-centric" reasons.

This is serious.

Beyond analysis, our experience dealing with entrepreneurs for more than twenty years gave us some knowledge we'd like to share.

It's not rocket science.

However, as these questions appear once and again, we thought it'd be useful to write them, just in case someone can feel relieved, at least feeling 'well, I'm not alone'.

Every question should have an answer, or at least a proposal, so that's what we intended to do.

I hope you'll be kind enough to understand we wanted to put some humor in these next paragraphs. We didn't want to mock or offend anyone. We've been in all these situations and suffered from them.

Having some fun and not taking ourselves too seriously is part of the road to any success.

Without further ado, these were some conversations we repeated once and again, in every sector, with entrepreneurs of any age, in different locations around the world.

Q1: Is now a good moment to start a new business?

No, there is NEVER a good moment to start a business. Let alone a perfect one. The good news is that there is not a bad moment to start a new business either. In a crisis, in growth, with crowded markets or only early adopters. With a busy labor market or with lots of talent available. When entrepreneurs want to check with us whether they have a good opportunity and timing, the only thing they want to hear is "yes, go for it," or "maybe not, I'd wait a while'. In other words: they want someone else to carry the burden of the responsibility.

When things go wrong, you'll hear many voices saying <u>Why a recession can be a good time to start a business</u>, showing lots of data about how big companies were born during tough times. Of course, we only know about the successful ones. Like for instance:

<u>Previous financial crises gave rise to high-profile American companies. The spread of the coronavirus challenges entrepreneurs to meet new needs.</u>

I found a nice quote that can be of help:

<u>Starting a business is similar to starting a relationship; the best time to start a business is when you have the time to devote your attention to it.</u>

Q2: What's the easiest way to overcome the instability and uncertainty of the first months/years?

This one's very easy. You cannot. Full stop. This is more or less like freelance writers / creators / YouTubers / podcasters / artists… Do not look at the stats. Just go. You believed in the idea. It would help if you showed you still believe in it. Who else would do that if you don't? 'Sometimes it seems we're stuck, like there is no way out.'

Keep pushing till you run out of whatever resources you have. And please, don't be dramatic; you did this because you wanted to. You drew a plan. Did you lose faith in a couple of months? 'I never thought this would be that difficult.' Ok, there are two impossible entrepreneurs types: the mentioned above, saying 'I gave up'. And the second, the one saying 'It was a piece of cake, success came so easy'.

Imagine the situation. You're not in the market, and then you arrive with a solution to a need no one knows it could be solved that way. No one knows. What do you expect? Having a long line in front of your door from day one?

Q3: I only can do urgent matters, how can I find time for my personal life and relax?

Bad news: your startup will eat up all the time you give it. And more. You can work twenty-eight hours a day, and it won't be enough; the next morning, you'll have even a higher pile of tasks to do—all of them burning on fire, of course.

Good news: as you'll never finish the tasks due, and your inbox will never go zero, it's your decision to stop whenever you want. Unless it's a life-or-death matter, it will be waiting for you tomorrow. And let's admit it: there's not that many life-or-death things as it might seem.

Some more good news: if you stop and exercise, see some friends, relax, spend time with your family, or just give yourself to boredom, you'll be a lot sharper tomorrow and will avoid a lot of mental problems later. Big problems today might seem small when you're fresh. And besides, a distressed mind and body will not warn you. It just goes or cracks. You should be in the driving seat.

Q4: How do I know I have the right partners in my project?

I can tell you the wrong reason to pick up a partner: because they're family or friends, or because they were there when you first talked about the idea. The good news is there's an antidote to committing this mistake: write a list of all the functions and responsibilities that every partner has assigned. They must be very clear ones, and they should be linked to the talents, capacities, resources of that person. Where you find a gap, you have a problem, and it's much better to have an awkward conversation at the beginning than having it when you lost a lot, and you're likely to lose even more (a friendship, for instance).

We need to have solid agreements, and very few but clear rules. We cannot imagine what could go wrong, but these things happen, and we'd better be prepared for the worse.

Q5: Will we know when it's time to stop, pivot, keep going, …?

No, we're sorry, you won't. There's no black or white in this. There are no right or wrong answers. Well, some dire situations could seem like the end, but… <u>no one knows when we'll have a plot twist</u>:

Ben & Jerry's almost got eaten up in 1984 when Haagen-Dazs' parent company, Pillsbury, threatened to pull its ice cream from distributors if they didn't drop Ben & Jerry's. When Cohen inquired about representation with a law firm, he was told it would cost at least $50,000—but Ben & Jerry's had only earned $7,000 more than that in net income the previous year. The partners launched the "What's the Doughboy Afraid Of?" campaign, distributing write-in kits containing letters of protest to the FTC and the chairman of the board at Pillsbury. On March 6, 1985, Pillsbury agreed it would not try to coerce distributors to drop Ben & Jerry's. In April of 2000, Ben & Jerry's was acquired by food manufacturer Unilever for $326 million.

Again, we don't remember the stories about the ones who did not make it.

Our advice would be to rely on different opinions and always have different views, as yours is going to be one hundred percent biased, and you won't see clearly. Let yourself be permeable.

There are hundreds of challenging thoughts crossing the minds of entrepreneurs every day, like imposter syndrome, financial problems, fear of failure, or stigmatization.

They should be admired, helped, supported, protected.

But the truth is that no one can take better care of them than entrepreneurs themselves.

Chapter 2
GO BACK TO BASICS: A FEW SIMPLE CONCEPTS, BUT PERFECTLY IMPLEMENTED

Keep looking at, and trusting, an updated version of the old concepts: mission, vision, value proposition, competitive advantage, business model, substitutes... At least, they will force you to ask a lot of questions, which in the end will be very good to have a healthier business.

Chapter 2
GO BACK TO BASICS: A FEW SIMPLE CONCEPTS, BUT PERFECTLY IMPLEMENTED

9. How To Improve Strategy: Drucker Will Make Your Day

Very few authors give you so many keys to a good strategy.

In my last article, I was talking about how to (re)define your company's strategy in these turbulent times, and someone made an interesting comment on how important is time and the way you use it. That made me think about having many discussion with companies about priorities, objectives, or resource allocation, which often end up me quoting one classic author. For me, one of the fathers of management thinking and one of the most useful and usable for everyday business life. Of course, I'm talking about Peter Drucker.

So, inspired by John Gruber and his article Science + Ben Franklin = Life Lessons, I decided to make my compilation of the sentences from Peter Drucker I use the most in my business (and even sometimes in my personal life) conversations.

So here we go, these are my favorites. If you want to add any, please feel free to leave your comments below.

Time is the scarcest resource, and unless it is managed, nothing else can be managed.

Some say that time is the most democratic and fair thing because we all have 24 hours, and we can use them however we want. That's true, in part, if we don't consider that the more money we have, the more time we can buy. But indeed, it is paramount that you spend your time according to priorities, know why you are doing what at every moment. I would add that even more important than doing what you want, is NOT doing what it's not in your priorities. Zero. Ignore it. Dump it.

Management is doing things right; leadership is doing the right things.

You could also change 'management' for 'efficiency', and 'leadership' for 'effectiveness', but the meaning is quite similar. Again, priorities are essential. Management (and efficiency) only care for doing something perfectly, but it doesn't question the purpose or meaning of that perfectly executed action. We'll come back to this in quote 10.

No one learns as much about a subject as one who is forced to teach it.

Have you tried that? Have you seen anyone trying to explain something, but he doesn't get through? It's like he does not understand, so he's not able to make it clear. It takes a considerable effort (and knowledge) to teach someone. You need to work on your communication skills, but first, the work of your subject. Corollary: don't try to teach anything if you're not an expert.

The best way to predict the future is to create it.

This one is also credited to Abraham Lincoln, but in essence, it addresses a very common deadlock in the companies. I don't know what's going to happen, so I cannot make any predictions (budget, sales, etc.). Don't look at it like this, but try to define your objective or scenario, and try to meet it and make it happen.

Strategy is a commodity, execution is an art.

There's another similar famous quote usually credited to Michael Dell. 'Ideas are commodities; execution is not.' Both go in the same direction: everyone might have a good strategy in the paper, but what makes a difference is the ability to turn that strategy into real results and achievements.

What's measured, improves.

I use another version of this one: if you cannot measure, it doesn't exist. The meaning is related to the importance of KPIs to show development, to check results, to encourage people, to know we need to adjust, to realize we're not going well.

The most important thing in communication is hearing what isn't said.

Experts in communication tell us all the time: words are only a small percentage of what every one of us is communicating. As well as doing nothing is a kind of action, what you don't say is usually as relevant as what you say.

We now accept the fact that learning is a lifelong process of keeping abreast of change. And the most pressing task is to teach people how to learn.

With all the technological development, knowledge society and Fourth Industrial Revolution, we're doomed to learn much, and learn fast. Some say that the only real critical ability for the 21st Century is keeping fit our ability to learn. Even learning how to learn is of crucial importance.

My greatest strength as a consultant is to be ignorant and ask a few questions.

I've seen many times consultants pretending to know more about the business than the company they are consulting. Wrong. It's much more challenging to listen, understand, and make smart questions, able to make the company think deeply about things they didn't see just because they are in front of their nose. Your best ability as a consultant is you know too little about the situation, and you're not impressed by the implications, consequences, etc.

And finally, my absolute two favorites, which I need to use al least once a week. This is quite personal, but I would recommend giving each one thought of five minutes.

There is nothing so useless as doing efficiently that which should not be done at all.

How many times have you seen a bunch of people in your company freaking out and as busy as it gets doing bull****? Think about it: should I be doing this? or should I be focusing my time on something else? I'm sorry, I'm busy. No, you decided to put your time somewhere else. It's your choice.

Business, that's easily defined—it's other people's money.

This one usually comes up when discussing business models and value propositions with entrepreneurs or more prominent companies. What's the reason why someone would open the wallet and give you the bill they have in it?

It is so effective, as everyone understands at lightning speed what we mean, and what they are supposed to do.

10. Don't Be a "Selfie Strategist"

Value proposition and business model are concepts usually misunderstood, but crucial for a good strategy.

Lately, I've felt that something's systematically wrong with the strategy of many companies and entrepreneurs. When revising and asked about their value proposition, companies answer once and again with the product. I tell them: "Now I don't care about the product; let's talk about your value proposition." Silence. Do you know what the value proposition is? Of course, I do. And then they rephrase the product again, with a different sentence.

Ok, let's look at it from another perspective. Do you remember Porter's Five Forces? Right. Give me an example of a competitor and a substitute. They name competitors. And a substitute? The answer is even more competitors, some slightly weird ones like they thought a bit more to the edge of the market.

–But you know what a substitute is, right?

–Sure.

–Give me a definition, just to make sure we understand the same.

–Well, now I cannot think of any.

—Don't worry; try to think about the value proposition of your competitors.

—Oh, yes, they are cheaper than we are.

—But that would be their competitive advantage, not their value proposition.

—Oh, isn't that the same?

This is a quite common conversation leading nowhere, and in the end, we let them rest. We try to remember that your value proposition is the NEED YOU SOLVE, not THE PRODUCT you put on the market. That's why a competitor is someone solving the same need with a product similar to yours, and a substitute is someone solving the same need with a completely different product. Like if you're stressed, you can go to therapy, practice mindfulness, go to the gym or go out to have some drinks with your friends. Or all together. Same problem (stress), same need (relax), many different substitute options.

Why do you need to think carefully about your value proposition

The value proposition is probably one of the most important concepts for a business because it forces you to get out of your comfort zone and put yourself in your buyer's shoes. When we reach this point, we tell the business to think about the value proposition leaving the "Selfie Mode" (my product, my solution, MY…). Our suggestion is to think about a situation when you can say to your client: "do not worry, forget it, I'll take care of it for you." In which context can you say this? That will be your value proposition. This may be even more important than your mission or your vision. Your mission and vision can also be inferred from the value proposition.

Let us put an example. Shopify does not say, "we are a platform where…". No. They say: "We build your online business—no matter what business you're in." Wow, can you do that for me? I'm a bit clumsy with technology, and I'm afraid of getting into tools I'm not sure I'll be ready to handle. I'm relieved you take care of everything.

You can even have multiple value propositions, like Amazon, which mission statement is quite famous, already: "to be Earth's most customer-centric company, where customers can find and discover anything they might want to buy online and endeavors to offer its customers the lowest possible prices." This mission derives to (or comes from; it doesn't matter) quite many value propositions, like "Easy to read on the go" for a device like Kindle, to "sell better, sell more" to its marketplace. Their products are intended to add value, but they are careful to explain that value in "your language," in terms which you can easily connect with.

How to build a good value proposition? In some very easy four steps:

1. Identify all the benefits your product offers.
2. Describe what makes these benefits valuable.

3. Identify your customer's main problem.
4. Connect this value to your buyer's problem.

The two last ones are probably the most important.

Not everyone has a stable and agile business model

Once you define your value proposition, one next (and key) step is being able to convert into a feasible business model. Again, we need to come back to basics, to what you understand as a business model. Often, there's a misconception about the idea, as many believe that your business model is only related to your revenue stream. But that's not complete.

There's an excellent reflection about how to define the business model at Harvard Business Review. It's not enough to say, "All it really meant was how you planned to make money," as Michael Lewis stated, but we need to go to sources like Peter Drucker's "assumptions about what a company gets paid for."

In short, we like the idea of a business model like how you get buyers to pay more money for your solution, than the money you spend to solve their need. The price must be higher than the cost. As simple as this. That's your business model. And for the same need, you can have many solutions (value propositions) and still many business models for the same solution. Imagine an online media that solves the public's need for information out of a business model based on subscriptions, on charging a fee for every content you want to use, on ads, or any combination.

"Selfie Approach" of strategy is the easiest one, but it's also one of the riskiest. Because you focus on your product, not your client, and if the market changes, you might not be aware, you may not be ready. Or even worse, you might not know what to do. The key, which value proposition synthesizes very well, is: don't think about what you can do; think about what you can do FOR ME.

11. The Need, The Product, And The Profit. As Simple As This

People have great ideas, but being able to turn them into a business is something completely different.

As Michael Dell said, "ideas are a commodity, execution is not." That's why any business idea (99% will fail, that's for a fact) needs to survive at least a couple of difficult conversations. After them, we can start taking them a bit more seriously and invest the time and resources to make them real.

In the beginning, though, many people are bringing us ideas we do not understand, or we cannot evaluate properly, because we're not experts in the field. After all, we don't know the market, or the potential customer, or the technical feasibility. But how do we know, then, whether we can be of help or not? We need to be sure we want to get involved in the idea, maximizing the odds of converting our time (and the time of the entrepreneurs, of course) into something meaningful and fulfilling.

Not being an expert in many fields, but knowing how to develop and grow ideas into businesses, we finally came up with a set of "filters" that has become a methodology to check, in a few hours, which could be the level of involvement and commitment with a project. We tested it many times, and for us is a very successful method to assess whether we will roll up our sleeves or run away as fast as we can. We're happy if it is of use for you, as an entrepreneur, or want to apply the methodology to any entrepreneurial situation.

So here we go.

Ok, tell me about your idea, but by the way, you need to create a company tomorrow

We put the entrepreneurs in "panic mode," telling them they need to start also with the annoying stuff asap. If the project has a few entrepreneurs involved, we ask them for some kind of partnership or shareholders agreement. Do you have one? What are the terms? They usually keep talking about the idea, and at some point, the question comes up: you're not going to copy our idea, are you? No, I'm not going to copy, and bear in mind you'll have to talk about the concept with a hundred different people. Do you have the skills to do everything on your own? If they are reluctant to talk about the idea and are unwilling to take real steps into action (legal, paperwork, etc.), it is probably a lovely bunch of guys talking about their s***.

How much money did you plan to invest in the development of the idea?

"We're already looking for investors, that's why we wanted to talk to you." Ok, fair enough, if you need 10 million dollars, it's likely you don't have it in your pocket, but what we are looking for here is a bit of commitment. A bit of confidence about the potential for the idea to convert into a successful business: if you're not absolutely sure (though maybe being wrong, we'll see) this is going to be a blast, who in the world would believe it so to put time, let alone money, in the project? Banks and investors smell fear, so you'd better be ready to ask many questions.

Tell me about your competitors

We don't have any; we discovered a blue ocean. No, seriously, never say that if you don't have a perfect explanation to keep going. Your assumption of being the smartest guy in the world, who realized first of an exciting opportunity no one saw, not even the potential costumers, could be ok to hardly anybody. So please, think about any potential company, business, team, product, or service that could serve the same need, or have a similar value proposition (we wrote about this in focus in another article). And of course, tell why we're going to be better. Here we need to refresh concepts like competitive advantage, which would be the subject for a probably longer conversation.

Show me you found a market willing to pay for the product you will develop out of the idea

This is a widespread mistake. We are so proud of the idea or the project that we don't remember that market does not give a s*** about what you're good at. They are looking for something to solve a need they have. If you provide it, they open the wallet. If you don't, they pass—that simple. So we're not talking about a lengthy market analysis with hundreds of different variables. No. Just show me that you have an idea about who is willing to pay for what, and this what is related to the product you're trying to develop.

Time to get into the product itself: tell me more details, how are you going to make it happen with quality and scale

If we assume we have potential clients waiting for us, we should be really good at solving their needs. Do you have what it takes to deliver your first thousand units? Next month? If you go blank or you start mumbling excuses, we have a problem. Processes, technology, and details are usually boring for some, but are crucial to any success. So I'm sorry, don't "fake till you make it" me. We need it solid.

Finally, the most important question: how much?

If revenue is not higher than cost, what you have is a nice hobby in which you spend money in exchange for satisfaction, amusement, or for killing time. But this won't be a business unless you're able to define a good and feasible business model. If you want investors, you will have to prove that numbers work, and how much work. So to say: how much money will I make with your project (AKA when will you make me rich?).

If you reach the end of the test, you're ready for almost everything. Well, at least you're prepared for the next steps, and you had the opportunity to pass your first stress test—

one of many to come. Show there's someone out there willing to pay for the product; show you know how to make the product happen; and show you know how to make revenue sustainably higher than cost. One, two, three. If, after that, you still believe in yourself, go for it.

12. Focus On Actions, Not Words

When you look at what people do, instead at what people say, you discover a completely new world. A more real one, we could say.

You should never ask your mother whether that wonderful idea you just had to start a new business is a good one or not. For many reasons, but one of the most important is that she loves you, she doesn't want to hurt your feelings, she'd tell you anything to make you happy. So, she would lie to you.

With your friends, your colleagues, your potential clients, may happen something similar. Maybe they don't love you, but often, they want to be polite, they want to save time ending the conversation (if they tell you they like the idea, you're happy and don't ask anything else); or simply, it's easier to agree than disagreeing and expose to your disappointment, or even worse, spark new questions you don't care about.

If you ask strangers or potential clients about your idea, things can get quite confusing too. Maybe they don't understand you (the picture is evident for you, but they are not familiar with it). Perhaps they genuinely like the idea, but they won't spend a dollar buying your product. Maybe they are just like your family and friends, who know that the best answer to the question "do you think the idea I had is good?" is a big YES. End of the story.

A brilliant book, The Mom Test, talks about the art of pulling information and preferences out of people, but without asking about you, but focusing on them. Where does it hurt? What makes you happy? Tell me about your life, your day, yourself. The only thing we all care about is ourselves.

The ton of social interactions we have every minute shows crystal clear that there are many poses and very few actions. Did your last post on any social media got hundreds of likes, thumbs up, applause…? I'm sure it did. But think it in some other way: did they do anything else than clicking? It's so fun when someone gives you a like, and immediately after sends you a pm with their last thing, asking to like and comment in return.

It's a pity, isn't it?

But we're wired to that, as Psychology Today explains:

"At a time when our ancestors shared the planet with woolly mammoths and saber-toothed tigers, no one wanted to get left behind. Group inclusion was necessary for survival. Today, our greatest predatory threat is our own species, both physically and socially. Regardless of this threat shift, the need for acceptance — and the fear that we won't be accepted — remain powerful influences on our thoughts and feelings. In fact, this in large measure fuels the existential anxiety that has become the hallmark of a generation, driving everything from people-pleasing to codependence to over-sharing on social media."

It's funny, right? Being liked is so rewarding that we stop and cut any possibility to develop and get better when we get it. And it can be worse. As presented in Scientific American:

"We too often think we are better at something than we are. Are you familiar with the Dunning Kruger effect? It holds that the more incompetent people are, the less they are aware of their incompetence. Dunning and Kruger gave their test subjects a series of cognitive tasks and asked them to estimate how well they did. At best, 25 percent of the participants viewed their performance more or less realistically; only some people underestimated themselves. The quarter of subjects who scored worst on the tests really missed the mark, wildly exaggerating their cognitive abilities."

Don't worry, there's a cure for that. We don't want to fall into complacence. We want to have real information about the outer world and our interaction with it.

Easy. When you'd want to know the truth, instead of listening to what people say, pay attention to what they do, each one of their actions. You'll discover an entirely new reality, probably a more real one. We are so sensitive to words, to believe them, that we often don't doubt even if our eyes are seeing the contrary.

I'll do everything I can to help you. Crickets. I'll find the time to get you a solution. Crickets. You can go on; you've lived dozens of situations like these in the past few weeks.

Ok, little white lies are all over, but don't let these take over your business. I'm not advocating for a Netflix-ish policy, or go the parody just like on Liar Liar, but we need to be aware when people are faking, posing, playing.

Not judging, just trying to get a more real, better version of the world. If you deserve no more than a like on Facebook, let's face it. If you're worth something more, go for it, call, touch, do. So as the song goes, "So sorry if I say some things I mean."

13. Key Success Factors Every Business Should Think About

> **Through our 20-year experience with businesses, we identified seven areas every company should check to know their odds for success.**

Over the past few years, I have seen many disoriented entrepreneurs. Some are in charge of companies that are doing very well; others are in projects struggling to survive. But no matter the level of success they'll achieve or have already made, they all share a common characteristic. Well, no, they share two.

For starters, almost every entrepreneur and are good professionals who are technically sound and have very reasonable business foundations. But **most of them don't know where they're going or what their priorities are**. They are running, running, running, nowhere. In a word: they are disoriented.

The latter does not mean that they have not made a business plan, detailed strategic planning, and do not have all the tools that, in theory, need to be born and grow a healthy company. They can even have passed rounds of financing and gained support and resources from investors. No, it's not that. It is merely that these tools have not been applied "for real." Therefore their strategy is written but empty. It was not created to pilot the company, but because they thought they should or, even worse, someone told them to. It is difficult to explain, but I am sure many of you know what I mean.

There are also cases where they've jumped into the market, relying on just a good idea. But that's another story.

In general, therefore, **it is relatively common to find entrepreneurs and companies without a strategic basis**.

And we are not talking about the easy parts –a document, a process, some objectives, a plan. No. We refer to what should typically come before the strategy, to what is usually taken for granted or "skipped": **the pure basics of the company.**

In our view, there are seven areas we consider paramount, which should be dealt with in-depth in any business project, whatever its dimension.

These seven factors seem essential for a company to have an identity and know where it is going. Some call them values; others call them skills or foundations. But in short, if an entrepreneur, an executive, if any partner or worker of a company is not able to respond fluently to these questions, they are at risk of not having a soul. This does not mean they cannot make much money, grow exponentially, or do reasonably well for a while. It will surely not have a clear identity, and consequently, they're at risk of losing its way of drifting at some point.

Many entrepreneurs show surprise when we ask them which ones are **the two ideas that make them able to answer all the questions in their company**. We see weird faces, and they quickly scan their brain for the chapter in the textbook in which they observed that part. No, in the book, there was no chapter for that; but later, they discovered their company could not do without these automatisms, which are part of the company's identity and culture.

We must bear in mind that the pace at which a company takes decisions increases exponentially with its growth. In the beginning, getting the first clients seems impossible, but the structure is simple in terms of management. But as soon as the machine starts operating at a relative speed, two fundamental aspects are put on a test: first, how people in the team can easily sync; and second, the ability of the company to make decisions at high speed in all its areas (productive, commercial, strategic, etc.). If the speed of action does not increase, it is impossible to grow and increase market penetration. And that is not only the strategy in the strict sense but a synchronization and fine-tuning of all the elements (tangible and intangible) that intervene in business development processes.

Below we have the list of the things we consider, according to our experience, to be aspects with a double condition: on the one hand, fundamental; and on the other hand, they are often scarce or absent, or we give them too little importance.

1. **The dream**. Every business project must have an engine, a spark that moves it with almost inexhaustible energy. A reason why it was created, the main objective, a utopia, a dream. And everyone in the company must know that dream and share it.

2. **The world**. It is surprising to see that there are companies that do not have a clue about the economic and social reality beyond their product, segment, sector, or market. Currently (due to the globalization of markets, the movement of public-private borders, the geopolitical situation, the technological revolution), it is essential to incorporate all the information and knowledge possible into our "production machine," not just from different sectors, but also from various disciplines.

3. **The foundations**. A company must have an ethic and an ideology. Not in the political sense of the word, but in the sense that it must have values, patterns of behavior, and an identity beyond its productive identity. You must have a clear idea, a commitment to a certain way of thinking and acting.

4. **The business**. It is also curious to see the surprised faces of many entrepreneurs when asked about their business model if they work if they want to change something. Although it sounds like a truism, a company must be a business. The result of any company must be positive in a sustained manner.

5. **The team**. People and their qualities are the main elements that make a company succeed. It is possible to start a business without money, but it is impossible to do it without competent and committed people. It may be that a family member or friend is a great travel companion for a business project. Still, it is not common, so the best option is for us to get a capable and motivated team to develop full confidence.

6. **The toolbox**. Today, it doesn't make much sense to think that what we learned at school or uni will be valid and enough for the next 45 years. Knowledge is no longer exclusive and compartmentalized, but we must understand it as pieces of a puzzle that we will unite so that they fulfill a particular function in the face of a specific situation or problem. The technique continues to exist, but the conditions in which we find ourselves

are no longer technical, requiring more complex solutions.

7. **The change**. It is a fundamental element of our new reality of the personal social, economic, and business structure of the 21st century. The transformation is constant, and therefore, the need for adaptation is permanent. Planning is still important, but knowing how to correct the course also becomes a fundamental variable. Are we prepared to change constantly?

If you cannot make it simple, nobody will understand. When it is not understood, it cannot be explained. And when it cannot be explained, we will not convince anyone. Zero sales. And if there is no story to tell, success can resist us extraordinarily.

14. Wy Business Fail? Is Your Company Making Lethal Mistakes?

Most of the times, bad leadership can ruin the right product

I'm not especially keen on talking about things from a negative perspective. I don't. I hate, I'm against. I don't like it; I think it's much better to build something from a positive point of view. I want, I wish, I hope. And it's not for any hidden, mistic, esoteric reason. It's because of such a pragmatic reason: I believe a "yes" has far more energy than a "no". In strategic terms, with a "no" you don't have a clue about where you are going, and besides, there's a risk for our brain to focus too much ib the think we don't want (remember the George Lakoff's book "Don't Think of an Elephant!"? Did you already picture the elephant?).

But sometimes, using an elephant analogy again, it's not enough to think in positive terms. We also need to cope with mistakes and do our best to avoid or correct them. In other words, we need to face the elephant in the room: 99% of the ideas will fail as a business. 60% of the companies created today will be dead in less than three years. Let's admit it: failure is the norm, and success the exception. However, we all want to be among the lucky chosen ones, though we know it is nearly impossible. So failing is a gift, one more step to success, an invaluable opportunity to learn, and all the stuff all the gurus squeeze into our brains. "Fail fast, fail cheap" mantra has become dangerously mainstream. It's ok to turn a mistake into a lesson, but please, do not convert failure into a goal. Being a professional of failure shouldn't be an objective or anything to be proud of. I read someone suggesting to change it for "Learn fast, Learn cheap." This one I like it better, thank you.

Ok, let's wrap up the idea. Accepting a mistake and learning from it is healthy, but try to make as few as possible. Does it make sense? Good, engrave it, then.

There are some situations you can see very often when a business fails. They are (unfortunately) extremely common, and dreadfully lethal. When you identify one of these in an organization, the best you can do is run away as fast as your legs can. Eventually, if you find some of them at the same time, the only thing you can do is facepalm, cry for a bit, and try to protect yourself from the detonation, because it may be very close.

We'll go top-down to understand how they can also be addressed. One caveat: the lower you go in the structure, the more difficult it is to change (as it involves changing deeply rooted behaviours of more and more people).

Let's have a look at them. I didn't mean to be ironic, but it's inevitable to fall for some irony. Fundamentally, we're talking about organizations that are sick, or not capable enough.

First things first: the product does not match any need

We have a great product, but no one understands. How is that possible? We're putting all the effort into developing the best, and customers do not care? We need new marketing, more money, more time. They'll eventually realize they have perfection in front of them, thank God.

Leadership is weak and based on fear, blind obedience, and wolf-pack loyalty rather than merit

Either you are with me or against me. Anything I did not build myself needs to be removed. The past is evil; the future is me. You're lucky I came. Micromanagement is a must in this organization because no one does the job better than me. Everyone is untrustworthy until they show otherwise and bow. Why everyone needs to be told what to do? I won't go on, you know the type.

You have a culture that punishes innovation

Innovation is taking risks to pave a new path. If you don't take any risk, you're not likely to get to any breakthrough innovation. And in many organizations, where "innovation" is a buzzword, the reality is much more inclined to "shoot'em up." I mean shooting anyone trying to think outside the box.

The majority of behaviours are defensive and excuse-oriented

Very much related to the previous one. It was not my fault, I did my best, but X screwed up. You cannot even imagine how much difficulties and pressure I'm going through. We have beautiful results considering the conditions in which we have to work. That's the best I can do without more resources. I need more everything, more people, more money, more time. And above all, a bit more respect, because I'm giving my life for this company and no one seems to care.

No one cares about anything but themselves

If you don't see any future in the company (for yourself, for the organization, for your team), the only option is to use it as long as it is alive, as a launchpad for your intentions and objectives. In the end, the only thing we can do is to loot the place until there's nothing left. It doesn't make sense to preserve anything, as nothing has any long term value.

No one smiles in a room

Some years ago, someone told me: do you know what shocked me the most when I arrived in the city? People were smiling on the streets. Have a look at some corporate pictures, events, enter a room and see their faces. No one's smiling? Worrying sign.

Honesty and integrity are optional; questionable practices are considered normal

Come on; it's no big deal. We've been working like this forever, and we survived. Ok, it should change, and we could do it better, but you know, we're probably not ready for that. Low self-esteem leads to losing values.

Focus is often in petty and wrong matters; gossip's a national sport

We build our strength on each other's weaknesses. I grow when you fall. I prefer to keep busy with tiny endless things than looking at the big picture. As Drucker said, there's nothing less effective than doing perfect something that should not be done at all.

There's a gap between the reality and the skills

On the contrary, you can also come across a healthy, enthusiastic organization where nobody knows what needs to be done. You can not build a productive and successful business without skills. We have excellent intentions, but not more than that. I'm sorry, mate, you won't last long. We need to come back to Peter's principle: if you perform well in your job, you will continue to rise the ladder until you reach the point where you can no longer perform well.

The obvious: operations suck

You promised the world, but you're not able to deliver— aka, dying by success. We're not capable of transforming our brilliant idea and product into happy clients. Things are usually more complex to execute than it seemed at first sight. Be careful, or you will never escalate.

And finally, of course: the financials do not work

Money can become a problem because we do not have enough, or sometimes because we have too much (from VC, for example) and don't know how to spend it properly.

This is like the second part of one of a previous article, **_The Need, The Product, and The Profit_**, but from our gloomy brother. Businesses fail because of bad leadership, dysfunctional teams, and bad execution. One wrong, and you have a lot to fix. Two of them wrong, and you're doomed.

15. Entrepreneurs Struggle To Come Back Stronger

Ask for help, work on your network, find mentors. And don't wait to do it when things get tough.

"**Sometimes it's ok to panic. For a while.**" This was the message James Basha, entrepreneur and motivational teacher, told us a few days ago, during a long conversation we had for our podcast *A Moment With*. It seemed a bit contradictory, but he said that asking for help is something we all should do more often. He knows well what he's talking about, because he's challenging, or "kicking their backside", many teams and companies around the world. With the pandemics, he moved online many of his sessions, helping the clients who are struggling in Europe, the Middle East, or America.

When something like this occurs, we need to understand we'll go through many phases. It is ok to get trapped, blocked; it is ok to feel lost. It is ok to panic, to get pessimistic, to ruminate going over and over the same negative ideas once and again, running around like a headless chicken. Many entrepreneurs and SMEs are used to live in this kind of rollercoaster most of the time. How do you break that?

You're mixing thoughts and positive and negative take over every minute. But after a while, you let the dust settle, and that's when you need to regain control and force yourself, bit by bit, to transform pessimism and reactivity into optimism and proactivity. The magic sentence is telling yourself: "I need to do things." When you can slowly do so, you realize that "if you remain optimistic and active, it is a matter of time that opportunities will appear again."

It's time to learn and invest in yourself, but at the same time, we should be aware that we will forget many of the things we're living in today. "We forget things quickly in order to survive" because we need to move on. But **this crisis is going to have permanent consequences, as it profoundly changed some of our habits,** and made us realize that changes were a must. Many companies are already talking about "Digital by Default," as they discovered that office and travel costs could drop dramatically without significant productivity loss.

The need for adaptation would be an urge, more than ever. Every company should force itself to think about the best strategy to evolve and keep competitive into the new context we're heading. Vision and purpose are essential for everyone, but especially for smaller companies, as bigger ones have more resources to manage tough times.

Don't wait for things to come to you. Still, at some point, you might be facing **one of the most challenging situations and decisions for an entrepreneur: you'll have to decide if you stop or not. Whether you quit or keep pushing, whether you pivot or say, "I've had enough, I'm done."** No one will take that decision for you, and no one can give you the formula to know when it's time to do it.

The only thing we recommend you do is: ask for help. Find a person (or a few) to turn to when you don't feel it. Work on your network and rely on people, but not only when things are not going well. Then it would be too late. That capacity should be built as part of your principles, your activity, and DNA as a company.

The cheapest and easiest way to get that help might sometimes be with someone who doesn't even know you. Someone you look up to, who has "been there, done that". It could be a leader like Nelson Mandela; what would he do in my situation? This could be a very powerful technique to find answers to your questions through exceptional "mentors."

16. Make Your Life Richer: Never Settle With First Impressions

The world today is a mighty current that could drag us all away. Don't go only with the tip of the iceberg.

Just like we have verbal and non-verbal communication coexisting with different codes in the same conversation, the obvious readings of the situations always include other possible, underlying, less transparent, sometimes hidden conclusions. Our brains can also get used to "reading" different levels simultaneously, just as it can get used to programming our actions so that they accomplish more than one objective at a time. Try it; at least you'll have fun.

Maybe one of the most popular ideas to describe this concept is the Plato's Cave, presented by the Greek philosopher in his work *Republic*. In this theory of perception, Plato states that reality is not what we think it is:

The cave represents superficial physical reality. It also represents ignorance, as those in the cave live accepting what they see at face value. Ignorance is further represented by the darkness that engulfs them because they cannot know the true objects that form the shadows, leading them to believe the shadows are the true forms of the objects. The chains that prevent the prisoners from leaving the cave represent that they are trapped in ignorance, as the chains are stopping them from learning the truth. The shadows cast on the walls of the cave represent the superficial truth, which is the illusion that the prisoners see in the cave. The freed prisoner represents those who understand that the physical world is only a shadow of the truth, and the sun that is glaring the eyes of the prisoners represents the higher truth of ideas.

Following the analogy, many shadows are thrown to us every minute, every second, coming from a thousand different directions, making it even more difficult to leave to cave and confront the "real world."

We should make an effort to go beyond the obvious and not stop at the first impression or interpretation when we read the news; when we have a conversation; when we think about a problem; when we try to solve a situation when we try to understand something or someone. Go always further, more in-depth, take one more step, try to see the light and not only the shades.

If the book "The Invisible Cities" by Italo Calvino has never fallen into your hands, I recommend that you search and look at it. Apart from being, as some wise man told me once, "the most beautiful book ever written on cities," it can also be a source of inspiration for many business projects.

One of the ideas that this book suggested to me a long time ago was that in reality, many aspects go unnoticed, invisible, but are often more important than others that make much more noise. And with the crisis we're going through, we are all a bit tortured with austerity, economic paralysis, and the daunting lack of institutional leadership. Companies and people show us day by day, their ability to continue surviving and advancing against all the odds.

A few days ago, in France, I met the owner of a small döner who had arrived from Turkey years ago, fleeing from a situation without any future. He had already passed through northern Italy, lived for several years in Poland, where he had a son, and now managed this small restaurant in France, hoping to come back to Italy to continue developing his dream as an entrepreneur. He spoke six languages (Turkish, Kurdish, Polish, Italian, French, and some German), but he has to change every day to keep moving forward. During my trip, I also met a growing French company, which has increased its workforce by more than 50% in the last year. Though, it sees how the business model will be exhausted in a short time and must also tackle an almost revolutionary process of change not to jeopardize their survival.

When you scratch a bit under the surface, in any country, you discover that almost everyone is continuously rethinking themselves, in a chameleonic way and increasingly dizzying speed. Change is no longer occurring every once in a while; it is no longer regular but an intricate part of our daily activity. And most people and companies, albeit barely, manage to keep up and improve their ability to adapt no matter what. Surely we will not get rid of this burden, but the good news is that many have already noticed and do not wait until it is too late.

Hopefully, the next time I go to Warsaw or Bergamo, I'll find the Mediterranean restaurant our friend from the döner wanted to open.

In the same way, when we plan our actions, we should always try to work quietly, steadily, and under the radar. With a lot of patience, taking into account all the conditions around us, of course, but avoiding distractions.

Above all, don't rush into anything. Reaching agreements against the clock is difficult, and usually leads to wrong solutions. In certain cultures, they say that business negotiations are brought to the point where your counterpart is in a hurry, forcing him to close more advantageous agreements.

That rush is never a good travel companion. In this sense, we must avoid being caught in situations where we have to make time-pressed decisions. Sometimes it is not so urgent; sometimes, the crisis must be allowed to precipitate. In many cases, whoever forces us to make a hasty decision has the objective that we are wrong.

In any of the motley markets of Northern Africa or the Middle East, we often find, apart from any object, some friendly salesperson blurting out a few words in your language, and also some other phrases that invite to deeper reflection.

"Haste kills," they say, referring to (and blaming) the permanent state of stress in which most of us live in the Western World.

It's nice to surf life; it's nice to have fun. But when it comes to important matters, your life will be a lot richer if you go under the surface, if you don't settle with the tip of the iceberg. Critical thinking is paramount; get out of the cave, see the light, and don't rush into anything just to go along with the crowd.

17. Time For Turnaround Management: A True Story

A big company was at a crossroads in the market, though still leading it. The CEO was humble and bold enough to call a meeting that changed the direction for the future.

The management team of a major multinational corporation in the food sector was quite concerned about the market position. That was why they decided to call a working day to discuss the situation and find some solution. They wanted to put their best minds to work together for a while. They were a group of about 20 people arriving at a small hotel away from the city, on a cold, rainy, foggy morning. They were looking somewhat concerned because they had been asked to go to that session without knowing very well the reason or the agenda for that day.

A cold morning

With the first coffee in the cozy meeting room, over a round table prepared for discussion, the CEO showed them the evolution of production and the latest results of the company, in which it was clear that the market share had declined significantly, even though they remained leaders, also indisputable.

They were one of the world's largest producers, though they were beginning to suffer very clearly from the impact of changes in consumers' perception and health habits. It started becoming evident that they could not go on with the same strategy and approach they held in the past.

In the words of the CEO, who carried out a very focused analysis from a correct (and sometimes too infrequent) self-critical perspective, the company had three main difficulties:

1. First, a leading product that had been there for decades, but heading towards a dead end due to market and demand trends.
2. Secondly, a competent and competitive technical and human structure, but very little used to innovation. The teams felt disoriented when they could not play a strong role, acting from its dominant position.
3. And finally, thirdly, a management team that, despite recognizing these trends, did not act accordingly. That was why they had been summoned to that day. It happened partly because of comfort, as they wanted to take advantage of their situation of personal and business privilege as much as possible. And from another perspective, they didn't know how to face the situation, lead the company to change, remaining at the same time a leader in that (or another) market.

Time for a big change

The challenge was to reinvent the company, the product, the culture the management. Change in capital letters. After a history of more than a century, guide profound change so that everything could remain the same. The challenge was to build a new strategy, developed from a new vision.

That challenge was both exciting and daunting. The CEO, and his small team of trusted people, had been warned that before trying to change an organization, you have to take the time to unfreeze it. They were referring to the well-known three-step model by Kurt Lewin (1946), who understood change as the modification of the forces that keep a system in balance. There are always two types of forces: those that want to drive change, and those that resist (usually represented in the status quo). Fundamentally, if we're going to change an organization, we must first unfreeze it. This step involves raising awareness of the need to change and removing or reducing any resistance. At the beginning of the process, the organization is balanced, and this first stage will, therefore, consist of clarifying the need for change so that everyone accepts it.

Moreover, any change and the CEO of our company knew it very well, requires much information, and created the necessary conditions. Sometimes we think that our sector, our competitors, our P&L, is the only important thing. But in an environment where technological and social change has become vertiginous, this VUCA world (Volatile, Uncertain, Complex, Ambiguous) forces us to take into account many more references than just two or three decades ago.

And at the same time, we must know how to organize all those trends and concepts and apply them to our reality. We must be able to analyze all this growing volume of information and turn it into a "What do I need?" so that change starts working as soon as possible in every corner of the organization. And we must bear in mind that it is increasingly difficult to impose changes.

There have always been great transformation strategies that have not worked because people did not believe in them, did not side with change. Reinvention must always be strategic, cultural, and organizational, but two fundamental dimensions derive from them, which will be key for a true reinvention to happen. First, teams must also reinvent themselves. And second, each one of us must do the same on a personal level. And if we do not move forward with our organization, we will inevitably end up going away from it.

Fear, leadership, and future

Therefore, it was reasonable that the management team of our company was restless, and that its CEO had to take the reins and lead trying to give certainties to face the challenge. During that working day, on a cold February morning away from the world in a small hotel in the middle of a forest, they concluded that they needed to create a team specially devoted to innovation and continually explore new ways to achieve competitive advantages. They decided they were indeed at a crossroads, even though their situation was not yet desperate, and that the moment required thinking about their business. In the early 90s, Lego realized that the toy market had changed and that they had to reinvent themselves profoundly (which took almost 20 years to find the new path). As at some point happened to Starbucks, or Apple, or so many other big, and not so big, companies.

From that day on, our company decided to take the first steps, knowing that if 75% of the organization is not pushing to reinventing itself, the transformation will probably never happen. They also created a new business intelligence and strategy unit, a small cell of five people already working at full capacity with the support of the board, and the enthusiasm of leading a profound transformation. They know that the path is not going to be easy, but that this is the only way that its future will not be in jeopardy.

18. Successful Entrepreneurs? Experience Is The Safest Way

Your first venture will not probably be the last. Get ready for a marathon; the resilient entrepreneur builds on experience more than in any other aspect.

Sometimes we do much science to show obvious things. "Entrepreneurs with a track record of success are more likely to succeed than first-time entrepreneurs and those who have previously failed," says National Bureau of Economic Research in their paper *Skill vs. Luck in Entrepreneurship and Venture Capital: Evidence from Serial Entrepreneurs*. Do they mean that the more you succeed (or fail), the higher the odds to be successful (again)?

Our empirical model indicates that entrepreneurs who succeeded in a prior venture have a 30% chance of succeeding in their next venture. By contrast, first-time entrepreneurs have only an 18% chance of succeeding and entrepreneurs who previously failed have a 20% chance of succeeding. This performance persistence suggests that a component of success in entrepreneurship is attributable to skill. While it may be better to be lucky than smart, the evidence presented here indicates that being smart has value too.

Wow. End of the story. The more you try, the "luckier" you get. I won't return to Malcolm Gladwell and his

Outliers' ten thousand hour practice to be proficient in anything, but this goes down to more or less the same idea.

The more successful, the more credible you are as you turn prior success into a public signal of quality and reliability. Therefore, the better money you attract, the better position you have in the market, the higher average investment multiple, so you sell equity at higher prices. And we start all over. Investors value experience, and investment often lead to success.

Thus, the idea comes down to two main questions.

First question: if I want to be a successful entrepreneur, I need to max the odds of success as early as possible (in my first, second venture?) so that the road gets much less bumpy ahead. How do I do that?

And here it goes the second question. However I can feel very talented for entrepreneurship, sort of like a natural entrepreneur, it also seems clear that skills count. And skills can be taught, in theory.

As Junfu Zhang from Clark University wrote in his paper _The Advantage of Experienced Start-Up Founders in Venture Capital Acquisition: Evidence from Serial Entrepreneurs_:

An entrepreneur may be born with **a general set of skills which he may then supplement by investing in human capital such as formal schooling**. He can also augment the set of skills through "learning by doing" in the process of building a firm, which is particularly important given that some entrepreneurial skills are subtle, uncodifiable, and difficult to teach in classroom. **Experienced start-up founders are expected to have a more complete set of skills and therefore perform better in their subsequent ventures**.

Learning by heart or learning from experience?

Your two or three first startups will be vital for developing your future career as an entrepreneur (or serial entrepreneur, if you prefer so). That's why you need to launch these initial ventures making sure you play with the best tools and in the safest environment. It's similar to life expectancy: if you survive certain thresholds, your life span gets longer and more stable.

So get in control, and avoid mistakes as much as possible. That's impossible, some may say, but we need to try. How? 1. Invest first in you, in your competencies and capacities; and 2. Get yourself closer and surrounded by those who can guide you through the journey of many obstacles.

So please make sure, when starting your first business, that you are entirely aware of your entrepreneurial skills level. Don't cheat on yourself. Be honest. Maybe it would be better to focus on and leverage your talents, but you also need to make friends with your weaknesses. Don't call it flaws if you don't want to, but you know those parts you struggle with that are boring for you, those you always procrastinate. Clifton Strengths could be a great tool to measure, but there are many. The question is that you must bring yourself to your highest potential, no matter how this potential is.

And after working with yourself, then you need to work to flow with the environment. To me, entrepreneurship is more an art than a technique, and that's why I think the only way to become an artist is to learn from them.

I don't mean some concepts and theories cannot be useful. I spend some of my time training future and developing entrepreneurs, and we emphasize the importance of ideas like value proposition, competitive advantage, and the likes. But after a couple of lessons, the most important for them is to start learning how to see problems coming, how to recover from a setback, how to manage some everyday situations. It's almost like "art transfer," like handing over the baton to new entrepreneurs with the successful ones' generosity to a new generation. It's much more about the experience than about information or knowledge.

So a training to become a trustworthy entrepreneur would today look like much more like a boot camp than a Master Course.

Not everyone is naturally talented to become an entrepreneur, and science has proven that you'll need to survive some real-life ventures before turning into a reliable one. From the very beginning, you should look at your journey as a marathon in which you will find many obstacles, and maybe being an entrepreneur is not pursuing a one-shot, but preparing to convert this into your professional profile for life. We don't mean being a serial is the only way, but you should probably address your career like that form the very beginning.

19. When Being Authentic Can Make You Successful

We analyze Ben & Jerry's business ingredients after more than forty years after being founded.

The story has been told a million times, but it doesn't mean it's no worth to give it another twist. We're sure you know about Ben & Jerry's. The origins, the growth, the values, the campaigns, the flavors.

But in a column like this, where we'll talk about people, we want to highlight personalities, traits, fashions, and WHY's behind companies (which are usually driven by people's minds and experiences).

Let's get rid of the popular stuff. Not because it's not important, but just because we all know about it:

In 1988, Ben & Jerry's was one of the first companies in the world to place a social mission in equal importance to its product and economic missions. Since then, the movement has grown and now has a unifying set of principles and criteria on which to evaluate socially responsible businesses.

You can have the whole story in just three minutes in this excellent video of Fast Company:

They care about democracy, racial justice, climate, LGTB equality, GMO, fair trade, refugees, and politics in general, among many other matters.

In a nutshell, they share the dream that one day, the companies will compete not to be the best in the world, but the best for the world. They say they operate on a three-part mission that aims to create linked prosperity for everyone connected to their business: suppliers, employees, farmers, franchisees, customers, and neighbors alike.

Why, after twenty years from a big acquisition, the brand has preserved its "social touch"? We have to remember that from "August 3, 2000, Ben & Jerry's becomes a wholly-owned subsidiary of Unilever. Through a unique acquisition agreement, an independent Board of Directors is created to provide leadership focused on preserving and expanding Ben & Jerry's social mission, brand integrity, and product quality."

Was that luck? Any secret from the past? A magic potion?

The first ingredient of the recipe is probably trust. Ben Cohen and Jerry Greenfield were childhood friends born four days apart in 1951 in Brooklyn. They were raised in suburban Long Island and met each other in junior high school. Big and small decisions can be tough, so you need to be in tune with the people around you. "I don't think we ever had a disagreement about money. The most famous disagreement was about the size of the chunks in the ice cream. Ben is well known for his inability to smell and, therefore, his inability to taste. So he was always focused on texture in ice cream. He liked big chunks of cookies and candies. But I was the one making the ice cream, and it's hard to put big chunks in ice cream. Ben was insisting on bigger chunks. Ben was right."

The second ingredient could be experience and the things you've lived. During his senior year of high school, Ben drove an ice cream truck. After high school, he attended and dropped out of various colleges in the Northeast, eventually leaving his studies altogether to teach pottery on a working farm in New York's Adirondack region, where he also dabbled in ice cream-making. Jerry attended Oberlin College to study medicine, working as an ice cream scooper in the school's cafeteria. He shared a Manhattan apartment with Ben. After moving to North Carolina for a few years, Jerry reunited with Ben in Saratoga Springs, N.Y., and they decided to go into the food business together. "We were both fat, dumpy kids growing up, and we liked to eat. So we knew we wanted to do something with food."

And here it comes a third ingredient: chance. It is very well known that they started first a bagel business. As they explained in an interview for The New York Times, "We were calling that business U.B.S., United Bagel Service. But we wanted to locate our business in a rural college town because that's the kind of place where we wanted to live. Eventually, we realized that there weren't that many people in rural college towns looking to have the Sunday New York Times and bagels, cream cheese, and lox delivered to their door. We actually priced out bagel-making equipment from a used restaurant equipment supplier, but we realized it was more money than we had between us. When we found out ice cream would be cheaper, we picked ice cream."

Of course, one more key ingredient. The product is important: Why has Ben & Jerry's been successful? "We usually say it's because of three things: really high-quality ice cream, great ingredients, very unusual flavors—and also the activist, social mission of the company."

A fifth ingredient would be time and resilience. For the first number of years, Unilever put its energy into integrating Ben & Jerry's into the Unilever system. During that time, the social mission of the company suffered. The company, as a brand, also suffered. But about ten years ago, Unilever named a new C.E.O., Jostein Solheim, and Ben & Jerry's rediscovered its soul. Failure is also part of the process for being successful, and that's probably why they have a cemetery for discontinued flavors.

They knew, or they made it possible, how to stand out from the rest, and we're sure that is due, to no small extent, to the personalities of the two founders. Ben & Jerry's, in many ways, embodies a challenger mindset in its industry. By challenging well-established brands and food industry conventions, the brand has boldly distinguished itself in just a few decades. And this strategy has worked so well because it feels completely authentic. Just like its founders.

20. Will You Take Care Of Your Relationships For A Longer And Happier Life?

The pandemic is posing threats to our relationships, but it is also giving us the opportunity to unleash positive and profound changes.

We're facing a new challenge. We still don't know if this will be permanent, or will slowly vanish and come back to "normal" after the pandemic threat. But relationships, social interaction seem to be changing really quickly.

This may be a social issue, even a psychological one, but what I'd like to talk here is about our health. As we know, the worse quality of your relationships, the more issues you're likely to have in your overall health levels. **Mens sana in corpore sano,** a healthy mind leads to a healthy body and the other way around.

This is science. Harvard study, almost 80 years old, has proved that embracing community helps us be happier and live longer.

"The surprising finding is that our relationships and how happy we are in our relationships has a powerful influence on our health," said Robert Waldinger, director of the study, a psychiatrist at Massachusetts General Hospital and a professor of psychiatry at Harvard Medical School.

"Taking care of your body is important, but tending to your relationships is a form of self-care too. That, I think, is the revelation."

"The key to healthy aging is relationships, relationships, relationships."
— George Vaillant

"Loneliness kills. It's as powerful as smoking or alcoholism."
— Robert Waldinger

One study? No, hundreds, as The Washington Post recounts in this article. How many more years of life we might gain by having true pals? Says lead author Julianne Holt-Lunstad, a psychologist at Brigham Young University in Provo, Utah. In an analysis that compiled data on more than 3.4 million people across 70 studies, she and colleagues found that the absence of social connections carried the same health risk as smoking up to 15 cigarettes a day. Loneliness led to worse outcomes than obesity. And the findings held true for people of all ages.

Quality counts more than quantity, Clinica Mayo says. While it's good to cultivate a diverse network of friends and acquaintances, you also want to nurture a few truly close friends who will be there for you through thick and thin.

Interested in getting deeper? Waldinger explains the results and implications of the Harvard research in a popular TED Talk.

So if the pandemic is putting us in a situation where we struggle to keep up with our relationships in a usual manner, like we used to do some months ago: will this influence our health and, ultimately, our life span?

The first thing we need to check is whether our relationships are suffering because of covid-19. Apparently, it is undeniable that face-to-face contacts have gone down dramatically, while online have been rising. We all complain that it's not the same, that we miss our friends, our professional environment, but how will it be when we "come back"? Will anything be changed for good? Kory Floyd, a professor at the University of Arizona, describes a concept called "skin hunger"—effectively, physical affection deprivation.

Indeed, those who relied mainly upon their work environment to cultivate their relationships are experiencing the first problems. In a research carried out in Australia, we see that those who relied on their workplace for social stimulation are more affected by the changes; those who had relatively good mental health before the pandemic reported greater changes to their mental health.

So, as in many other aspects of the situation we're living, we'll only see the real impact when we overcome the critical phase. Only then we'll know whether these consequences will be temporal or to what extent they will permanently transform our habits and behaviors.

It's exactly the same as we will experience with remote work. Let's wait for the dust to settle, and then we'll see what changed in the picture. What we know for sure, in both cases, is that the long term impact will be certain and significant. In a word, our world is changing, and it's doing it at fast-forward speed.

As The New York Times explains, with the coronavirus lockdowns, many of us now have more time. Maybe we aren't dressing in the morning, commuting to work or meeting pals after office hours. Many of us have more time to talk. Moreover, we have something important to talk about. Have chitchat and small talk become far less relevant?

But coronavirus outbreak put our relationships under a lot of stress, and our connections are being reshaped, especially the closest ones. Life in lockdown has necessitated close, constant contact with our families and partners, but social distancing measures have isolated us from our friends and wider communities.

This means some of our most important relationships are under great pressure. BBC reports that there is most evident in a spike in divorce rates. In Xi'an's city in northwest China's Shaanxi province, marriage registration offices saw an unprecedented number of divorce requests when they re-opened in March.

Experts say isolation doesn't have to be a bad thing. Time in quarantine, whether it means spending more time together or less, could be an opportunity to strengthen your relationships.

But experts also say that we'll be less touchy-feely and far warier, but the transition will feel strange. Distance between people, either physical and psychological, seems very likely to remain in our new reality. And this will probably lead to a bigger difficulty to create bonds. We've been practicing social distancing for months, keeping at least two meters away from each other, avoiding touching communal surfaces, and stifling coughs and sneezes. It has been difficult to quash a lifetime's experience of learned societal norms that demonstrate politeness or affection: in many cultures, we shake hands when we greet new people, hug those we care for, or offer a hand, literally, to those who need it.

But yes, now we've become wary in almost any social interaction, or even in any public space like shops, restaurants, or transport. Will this feeling last, leading to lower levels of trust in our everyday life?

Shall we turn all this situation into an opportunity to change our relationships for the better? Our future health may depend on it.

Chapter 3
YOU CAN'T DO IT ON YOUR OWN: TEAM UP!

In the 20th Century, the keyword was (hashtag) competition; the most important thing was to win, to beat the opponent. The powerful position was the pyramid's cuspid, and the higher you climbed, the harder the wind blew.

Things have changed in the 21st Century. The keyword is (hashtag) cooperation, or collaboration. The magic potion is the network. It's time to share and harvest the value of collaboration. The most powerful position is in the nodes of much more horizontal structures.

If we called capitalism to the economic system born out of the first Industrial Revolution, the economy and society we are building today should probably be called Networked Technology Era. The Age of Networks, or something similar.

And guess what? People will surprisingly remain to be at the center of this new paradigm. Because we're still necessary to make the world go round. At least, for a while, we'll see what the 22nd Century brings.

Chapter 3
YOU CAN'T DO IT ON YOUR OWN: TEAM UP!

21. Cooperation Is Always The Best Option, In Business And Life

We should remember that cooperation brings the best results for a group, even though it might not make you rich.

We already discovered, through the biopic "A Beautiful Mind," the disturbing story of disease and genius about one of the most brilliant scientists of the 20th century. Unfortunately, the mathematician and Nobel laureate in economics John Forbes Nash passed away five years ago, but he left important economic science contributions.

Usually, mathematics and economic theory are not part of the media headlines, but that doesn't mean that they could not explain much of that news. The so-called "Nash Equilibrium", formulated by the mathematician, offers us valuable keys to understand numerous behaviors in economics, politics, and geostrategy.

It's discouraging when we see world leaders fail to reach agreements at climate summits, conflicts, trade, or pandemics management, which would benefit the entire world population. It's sad when we see that governments allocate greater budgets to defense than anti-poverty or equality policies. It isn't easy to understand when the metropolises live collapsed by traffic while much more efficient forms of public transport could be developed.

It's unacceptable when many political parties and institutions behave exclusively seeking their interest and benefit, knowing that they must be committed to pursuing the general interest.

There are situations when countries decide to borrow far beyond their ability to repay that debt, literally mortgaging the future of the following generations. In the meantime, some companies decide to pursue their shares to skyrocket as fast as possible, even at the cost of their strategy and their future sustainability.
We should think about the actions of multilateral organizations, such as the International Monetary Fund, when they impose conditions they know will ruin those who have to meet those requirements.

These are only a few examples. We could go on with so many other examples that show why all those people, governments, companies, and institutions act in such an incomprehensible way; why are their decisions so openly marked by individualism, selfishness, self-benefit, and survival the only motivation?

Let us come back to the Nash Equilibrium, formulated in the late 1940s in the scientist's doctoral thesis. He was influenced and attracted by John von Neumann's Game

Theory, with whom he met at Princeton University. In summary, Nash formulated that a 'game' ends when each player, independently, chooses his best response to his opponents (which replaced with scientific reasoning the "Invisible Hand" of Adam Smith).

One key aspect of this formulation is that it "proves" that collaboration between players never leads to a balance. Situations evolve naturally towards the best option for each player, never towards the best option for all. Surely you have heard of the "Prisoner's Dilemma."

Are we doomed to wild competitiveness even though we know that we are going against a better collective solution? Well, no, we shouldn't. Nash Equilibrium also shows that the option to collaborate always offers better results for all players, but unfortunately, the individualistic option minimizes losses.

This entire chain could be broken, in theory, if the players decided to collaborate. And keep their agreements, of course. Could that be possible? Indeed, it would be a revolutionary economic and social change. Have those who are currently negotiating politics and economics around the world heard of the Nash Equilibrium?

22. Do The Magic To Be In A Great Team

When a team does not work, we usually see only the symptoms. Try to go to the root of the problem to turn a dysfunctional team into a happy and productive one.

It gets really tiresome. We all have lived in one of those teams full of gossip and lies to cover weaknesses. The nice, the smart, the dumb, all the roles of the play, like a small world or family. How many days have you spent solving silly conflicts? How many times did you get mad because someone is behaving childish, or selfish, or mean?

Sometimes your boss puts the Peter Principle in the flesh or you catch your colleague stabbing the teammate to get up the ladder. You know the guy who sends an email bomb and then ghosts as if nothing happened. Hey, this happens everywhere, it's human nature. You know what? Settle for this may be the beginning of the end. Of the team, I mean.

Did you ever dream of being part of a fully functional, stable and balanced team? It's not a utopia. And the best thing about it: it's not the teams' fault. All those behaviors are just symptoms, not necessarily a disease. The team is sending signs that need some fixing. Most of the time, it doesn't even require letting people go, but just an alignment.

(i) Start by naming the problem: the five most common team dysfunctions

Patrick Lencioni is an American writer of books on business management. He is best known as the author of *The Five Dysfunctions of a Team*. The first step towards reducing misunderstandings and confusion within a team is understanding that there are five dysfunctions and that each one that applies has to be addressed separately.

Namely:

1. **Absence of trust**: The root cause of absence of trust lies with team members being unable to show their weaknesses; to be vulnerable and open with one another. The absence of trust is a huge waste of time and energy as team members invest their time and energy in defensive behaviors, and are reluctant to ask for help from or assist each other.
2. **Fear of conflict**: Teams that are lacking trust are incapable of having unfiltered, passionate debate about things that matter, causing team members to avoid conflict, replacing it with an artificial harmony.
3. **Lack of commitment**: People will buy into something when their opinions are included in the decision-making process. This is not as much about seeking consensus but making sure everyone is heard.
4. **Avoidance of accountability**: In a well-functioning team, it's the responsibility of each team member to hold one another accountable and

accept it when others hold them accountable. Very often, the key to success is the measurement of progress: making clear what the team's standards are, what needs to be done, by whom and by when.
5. **Inattention to results**: Teams can overcome this dysfunction by making the team results clear and rewarding the behaviors that contribute to the team's results.

(ii) What's behind the symptoms of a dysfunctional team?

As a strategist, I've been working with hundreds of different teams through more than twenty years. My experience is that all these **dysfunctions usually appears because of to main reasons: toxic corporate culture, or bad leadership**.

With regards to culture, by the way, where is your team in this diagram?

And in terms of leadership, I like Simon Sinek's approach. *"You're responsible for the people who are responsible for the results."*

What makes a great leader? it's someone who makes their employees feel safe, who draws people into a circle of trust. But creating trust and safety—especially in an uneven economy—means taking on big responsibility.

Does it look like your boss?

(iii) How to make your team functional

One of the most outstanding research about teams carried out during the last years has been called Project Aristotle. Google spent two years studying 180. Specifically, they wanted to know why some teams excelled while others fell behind, and they discovered the most successful ones shared five traits. As presented in a New York Times very popular article:

After looking at over a hundred groups for more than a year, Project Aristotle researchers concluded that understanding and influencing group norms were the keys to improving Google's teams. But Rozovsky, now a lead researcher, needed to figure out which norms mattered most. Google's research had identified dozens of behaviors that seemed important, except that sometimes the norms of one effective team contrasted sharply with those of another equally successful group.

Google presented the results, hihghlighting those five traits:

The researchers found that what really mattered was less about who is on the team, and more about how the team worked together. In order of importance:

- **Psychological safety:** Psychological safety refers to an individual's perception of the consequences of taking an interpersonal risk or a belief that a team is safe for risk taking in the face of being seen as ignorant, incompetent, negative, or disruptive. In a team with high psychological safety, teammates feel safe to take risks around their team members. They feel confident that no one on the team will embarrass or punish anyone else for admitting a mistake, asking a question, or offering a new idea.

- **Dependability:** On dependable teams, members reliably complete quality work on time (vs the opposite—shirking responsibilities).
- **Structure and clarity:** An individual's understanding of job expectations, the process for fulfilling these expectations, and the consequences of one's performance are important for team effectiveness. Goals can be set at the individual or group level, and must be specific, challenging, and attainable. Google often uses Objectives and Key Results (OKRs) to help set and communicate short and long term goals.
- **Meaning:** Finding a sense of purpose in either the work itself or the output is important for team effectiveness. The meaning of work is personal and can vary: financial security, supporting family, helping the team succeed, or self-expression for each individual, for example.
- **Impact:** The results of one's work, the subjective judgement that your work is making a difference, is important for teams. Seeing that one's work is contributing to the organization's goals can help reveal impact.

You can have a closer and deeper look at all the results in the original website, but it can be summarized in this diagram:

So the next time you see your team does not work well, or you're worried or annoyed by any sticky behavior, remember that you can analyze all these aspects and try to change the situation, step by step. As you're dealing with people, it's not going to be easy whatsoever, but at least you can focus on fixing small things (or big ones) to achieve much better results.

23. Unmasking The Fake Entrepreneur

Tip: you won't find in them any sign of generosity.

Someone approached me last week. He was a Fake Entrepreneur, and he had a supposedly great idea for a new business. I listened, and I thought the concept could even have some potential if we could take care of every detail, doing it fast, thoroughly, and honestly.

In the beginning, it's virtually impossible to identify a fake entrepreneur, but you could work your way with some quite simple steps. It's difficult to know because they look active, creative, they have some kind of contagious energy. They have already done some smart work; they have taken some actions, making the whole project seem to be in the right direction. It's your time, then, to take one step back and look at all the items at the same time, ask the questions an investor would do, and put on the table those aspects that would be the concern of a COO.

I usually say that I don't pretend to be an expert on everything, every sector, every product. Maybe I wanted to some time ago, but not anymore. Your only aspiration should be to ask the best questions about the project and sometimes try to help find answers. Here's where the Fake Entrepreneur gets exposed. Naked.

Ok, we didn't give a definition yet. What are we talking about when we refer to a Fake Entrepreneur? This is probably the most dangerous species for a healthy and sustainable entrepreneurship ecosystem. They are the ones creating bubbles; maybe we had too much of them during the latest ten years, and that's why we are on the verge of discovering that just a tiny (really tiny) percentage of ventures can be a unicorn. It's just like everyone was sure they would get the big prize in the lottery.

If everybody is a unicorn, no one is.

The Fake Entrepreneur, you'll see that quickly, is the one having all the answers. They are the ones who don't care about the product, the quality, the detail, but they focus much more on pretending they are real, with an unbelievable trust in being successful. The worst thing about it is that you're lame if you raise any questions or concerns. "Maybe you shouldn't be in the project if you don't trust it." No, no, don't get me wrong, please. What I don't trust is not the project; it's you.

Because in the end, ventures are about people. You believe in a project because of people, never because of the idea.

We're lucky because you can recognize the Fake Entrepreneur. After all, they share a particular and clear trait.

They are or try to be charming. If they really are, this could be a "false positive," but if you see any sign of greediness or insecurity behind the charm, start running.

They pretend (or even try) to be open-minded and active listeners, but they are not. Just check whether they remember anything you told them, and besides if they behaved in some way according to anything you said. With a Fake Entrepreneur, you'll never discover anything yours in the projects. They don't want partners; they want soldiers, sometimes slaves serving their own purposes, and it's common that they patronize you. They allow you to be in their project; it'll never be yours if you don't follow their orders. "Could you do that for me, please?"

They can become dismissive but rarely aggressive, especially if they want to cultivate a reputation. They'll push you to put many resources into the project for the sake of creating an image of success. That's probably the main thing you need to look for to unmask a Fake Entrepreneur: they prefer success to anything else. They will find achievement on anything, and they will claim it to be their own.

That said, it's quite obvious they are incredibly selfish, even narcissistic. This is a complicated point because the balance between having the irrational faith needed to grow a successful project requires much self-assurance. Every entrepreneur has the potential to become a narcissist, and it's your job to keep this "natural talent" under control and only serving a purpose, not "your" purpose.

Therefore, when the conversation goes to money and rewards, they always deserve and will get the lion's share of everything, especially when it comes to significance. They had the idea, they found a way to make it happen, and they had the ability to get the best team (you) onboard.

They may not be psychopaths, but what you'll never find in them is any kind of generosity. Quid pro Quo is their religion, the only behavior they understand.

Their policy is: "Thank you? No, you owe me."

There's no "i" in a team, neither in an entrepreneur.

But the Fake Entrepreneur can drag anything or anyone for the sake of its own glory. You'll never work with them, only for them. If you don't want to get into that, don't think you can change them. Run as fast as you can so they can get you.

Maybe we could call them Intrepreneurs.

24. The Power of Being Normal

Melanie Perkins, the founder of Canva, shows the power of a cool entrepreneur who can be the third wealthiest woman in Australia while still having her feet on the ground.

The story could be one more of those of youngsters pursuing their dream. She remembers pitching more than a hundred people in less than two months in San Francisco, far away from her home city, Perth, in Australia. She dreamt big and started small, as many do. She wanted to entirely change the desktop publishing industry when she was 19.

You've probably heard from her. Her name is Melanie Perkins. She created one of the tools that maybe you're already using to make your presentations look fantastic. And Canva is today it's a billion-dollar business (if you want to know more about her story explained by herself, you can listen to the podcast episode How I Built This where Guy Raz has a really nice conversation with her).

People with no design experience sometimes need to create something that looks professional. We don't know where to turn to. Melanie thought about her mom, a teacher, who had to create student yearbooks, and started from this.

She and her boyfriend took a fifty thousand loan from F&F and hired some developers to get started with building web-based design software, although they didn't know how to code whatsoever. And then, a Silicon Valley investor was at a conference in Perth in 2010, and serendipity happened. Perkins met him, and everything started to go big when she went to Palo Alto with everything she had put together for her most important pitch so far.

Fast-Forward, ten years after that meeting, to make a long story short. Today, the startup value is around six billion dollars, two times the valuation of less than a year ago. Its latest round of funding makes Canva the largest privately-owned company in Australia. The now Sydney-based company, with more than a thousand employees, operates across multiple countries. It has a "freemium" model that allows its users to access its software for free to design hundreds of products, including posters, websites, and business cards. Design creation and sharing on Canva have increased by 50% since the start of COVID-19. They are doubling its paid user base, which has reached over half a billion organizations and 1.5 million paid subscribers to the paid account type, Canva Pro.

Twenty designs are created in Canva every second.

Perkins has become the third wealthiest woman in Australia and the youngest Aussie billionaire. Her personal wealth has been estimated to be around $1.3 billion.
All in all, behind the numbers, there's always the person. In an interview, she recalls when she met Lars Rasmussen, who co-founded Google Maps, she thought he was "just" a nice normal person who worked really hard. At that moment, she felt empowered and changed her perspective on what was possible.

"When you think we're on a planet with seven billion other people, it's very easy to think that surely someone else has more experience, more knowledge, more power to help improve this world. But it's a pretty frightening realisation that we are on this planet with seven billion other first timers."

Melanie's also generous with her time, penning a lengthy and technical post on Medium, answering 21 questions from the startup community on her startup's journey until now, offers some lessons, details the ups and downs, and outlines how she deals with the pressure. The company is passionate about philanthropy and contributes significant donations to the causes the founders care about. Last December, Perkins announced that Canva would join the 1 percent movement, donating 1 percent of its equity, profit, and resources to "making the world a better place."

"We believe the old adage 'do no evil' is no longer enough today and hope to live up to our value to 'be a force for good'."

She sounds humble; she looks authentically normal, grounded, balanced. In her early thirties, she's still with that boyfriend who shared her dream a decade ago, and now they are named to be one of the most important "power couple" in Australia. She is proud to support 25,000 nonprofit organizations that use Canva for fundraising.

Honestly, it is refreshing to see someone up there and, at the same time, so down-to-earth. Hopefully, she could be a sort of role model for a whole generation of new entrepreneurs.

25. How To Choose The Best Investor For Your Company

Some tips to make decisions you won't regret

When having conversations with entrepreneurs, some of the questions and topics are often alike. That's why I asked a friend for permission to publish a summary of our latest discussions, hoping they may be of help to anyone in a similar situation.

I am working for a start-up company right now, and we have two potential investors.

First, and probably the most important thing, is how do you want to spend the money. As a company, you need to know where every cent will go, for many reasons.

First one, because when you start spending the money, you must have tight control over allocation, efficiency, timing and milestones, deviations, KPIs and results, impact, further needs, or any adjustment that we should implement on the go.

The second one, because as an investor, I need to be sure my investment is coherent and makes sense. Let me put an example. When a start-up developing a new app or web service, wants to put 90% of the investment to marketing, and 10% to product development, we have a problem. Or the other way round, if we want to invest 90% of the resources to secure an IP (patent, for example), we've also a problem. With these examples, I mean that we should have a coherent investment structure. And of course, a coherent volume. Because if a company of a 1 million pre-money valuation asks us for a 100 million investment, maybe we should also be a bit worried.

Third, because investment must be coherent with the product, with the team, the market, and the context. In this case, the type of business will lead the way for many of the checkpoints. It's not the same if you are a scientist asking for an investment to develop an industrial prototype out of a new invention, or if you are developing a new website or marketplace. Imagine you're investing in that industrial prototype, and the founders don't have the technical ability to negotiate the terms with a contractor, or they don't have the connections to make that prototyping possible.

In short, we need to have a clear direction, a reasonable approach, and credible plans and numbers. You don't need to have a detail up to the last cent, but you need to be ready to answer any question. So better you did in advance as many questions to yourself, and you've been able to convince yourself first with good answers. In the end, you want to provide some certainties to you and your investors, and some feeling of security for everybody's money (or at least, some control over risks).

The first investor wants to give Cash for Equity and participate with know-how and helps us with sales.

We need to remember a couple of things here, which are paramount. When you think about the easiest deal-breakers, these two ones often come to mind.

First, the valuation is critical. We need to agree on the value of the business, because, of course, this will decide how much equity you can ask for your money. Methods are numerous, though, in many projects, very few are used. But the question, in the end, is how much do you think the business is worth. And it relies on a thousand different variables, but the three main ones are: product, team, and luck. Concerning the three of them, both parts (founders, investors) may have a different perspective. So when you are talking about the percentage of equity you're giving away, the real discussion is 'will you give me 10x somewhere in the future?'

And second, the value (or price) of the investor's contribution. You talk about "know-how and help in sales'. Ok, what are precisely these functions? Are you buying your job? Or are you accelerating your investment? Maybe you are helping because we get along well? To my experience, it's always good to name names and to set things apart. I put X cash, and I want X equity for it. On the other hand, I add this value to activity, equals this amount of money at market price, and I want an extra X equity for that. You can even say that I'm the first fool believing in your idea, and I'd also like to have additional equity for that. It's ok, everyone can ask for whatever he wants, but as a company, we need to know what we are paying for. And every investor would agree, would thank, and would be happy with that policy.

This one looks more like an individual investor, willing to put some engagement in the development of the project. But in these cases, as a company, we need to measure the ability of this type of investor to walk the talk, and effectively add value to the business. This kind of relationship implies some amount of trust between the parts, mostly related to people's bonds.

The second one wants to give a convertible loan, that they can convert into equity after three years. Having them participating would add a very well known name to our board.

This proposal looks a bit more professional, and the formula has become more popular for seed investment. It can be quicker than selling equity, cheaper, and the control about decision making remains mostly on the founders (as equity investors usually have board seats, some veto rights, and things like participation preferred liquidation preference). It provides many options (a coupon if the loan is finally not converted, for example), and gives you richer tools to negotiate in later rounds. Of course, there might be some disadvantages too, like the fact that founders want to maximize the company's valuation in Series A, while the noteholder's interest is to minimize it.

Concerning the second point you mention, it's interesting that this second investor is adding value to your project (co-branding) without any need to perform any action.

What would you say with whom to go within that case? Or would you see other options that we can propose to get the two investors on board? The second one is unlikely to also invest in equity from the beginning.

Founders are usually afraid of equity investors, because they dilute at a sensitive moment (at the beginning, when everything is still uncertain), and because they lose control over 'their baby'. It's safer, because you don't need to pay the money back, but things change a lot when investors come.

In the real world, a combination of different sources are always probably the most sensible option. Because you diversify the risk, you get many more on board, and if you need any loan in the future, it's easier if the banks see more people believing and invested in the project.

My advice, in this case, would be to prioritize the second investor, taking into account that you might have another one (the first). I would negotiate to get both on board, as the more people the market sees involved in the project, the more attractive you are going to be for everyone. Work on a plan and investment details. Build a valuation that you believe in and go for it. The most important thing is for you to have your own goals, and you find a good match; don't work the other way round. Be ready to see things differently and to pivot, but I would not 'sell' the idea to the first arriving just because they show interest and pledge to put some money on it.

Do not rush into anything. Especially now. And do not sign anything that you think it's not fair or reasonable. A good deal may be quick, but it isn't easy to sign a good one in less than six months. My experience is that the faster you sign, the more "winners and losers" situation you have, and this means trouble in the future, for sure.

26. Forget About Quantity, Good Networking Is Based On Quality

How long since you made your last meaningful professional connection?

Here's an entrepreneur talking. You know you must attend a thousand different events, be active in social media, be present, cultivate relationships with partners, clients, peers, stakeholders. You need to have a reputation, build a profile, and be consistent with it. You have a big HR manager for yourself, which is called the market. In the end, you live in an environment, in a network of networks in which is easier than ever to find new connections. But in which is also as difficult as ever to turn those into MEANINGFUL ones.

You know that probably 80% of that time will be useless, of absolutely no value (maybe Pareto might also be applied here). But you need to show up, just to come across the 20% gems out of the whole activity.

Linkedin, as the central hub/market to accomplish this kind of networking functions, may be considered a reasonably efficient tool. But maybe it's mainly a useful tool for quantity. So we would like to know what your feelings are about your network, whether you think about it, and act about it on purpose. And in short, how is your effort, and how you feel your results reflect that effort. Are you happy with the management of your professional network?

Do you prime quantity over quality? What are you looking for?

It seems that to be a star, what it takes is to have thousands of connections, even though you do not have a close personal relationship with most of them. Sometimes it makes us think whether we are looking for links or followers. Do you know everyone in your networks? Or are you accepting invites just to enlarge your reach? Especially at Linkedin, are you building a network or a showroom for your reputation? Do you read many posts from your connections and react? Are you genuinely interested in your timeline, or just expect others to be interested in yours? What would happen if tomorrow half of your LinkedIn connections disappear?

Where do you find your most trustworthy partners and connections?

Sometimes they say that a club on a Friday night is not the best place to find someone to marry. So are social media the place to find meaningful connections? Or just a marketplace for fast food? Sometimes you realize that you are not connected in social medial with someone essential for your network. Do we need other spaces for the relevant people? And in this sense, when you try to find a new connection for any purpose, where do you go? Do you jump from one tree to another to cross the forest, or you just go to your phonebook and send a PM to find a trusted opinion and jump safely?

Do you have a strategy to manage your network?

Does your network grow organically, or you developed a plan to feed it conduct its growth? Do you just rely on luck or any specific need, or you try to build it consistently, brick by brick? If you turn your sight to the past, are you happy with the development of your network? Would you do anything differently? Do you think social media has changed the way we connect and the shape of our networks? Or are we just in an online "business as usual" scenario, in which technology is only one more tool to do the same we did? Do you purposely apply criteria to enlarge the scope of your relationships? Do you hand-pick your objectives and pursue these connections through different tools and means? Do you have some kind of mental or technical CRM to take care of your contacts?

What's the percentage of "peer to peer" in your network? How do you address "different levels," up or down?

The majority of our network is composed of "peer" members (I couldn't say a number, but the percentage may be higher than 75%). Similarly, most of your close relationships are in a range of 10 years up or below your age. But connections up and down the ladder may be essential for your development, too. Sometimes we only think about the ones who can get you to levels you cannot reach so far. We think about people who are already higher or more prominent than we are, mentors, C-level executives, shareholders, or big investors. But it's also essential to build a reliable web of connections in other environments, those who could be of value in many different senses. How do you work on those types of relationships? Do you find it easy to go to not so "natural" connections to you? Do you use the same methods or techniques for these connections than for the rest?

Do you work a lot offline to build and take care of your network?

In the age of technology, how important is it still the offline world for your network growth and hygiene? According to many HR experts, word-of-mouth is the top option for many recruiters to fill in more than eighty percent of the jobs, especially in headhunting. So many of the posts never really go public in the work portals, and the higher the skills, the lower the public visibility, and the more opaque and fenced.

I'll give you my perspective and reflections on the issue. I think that networks, especially when it comes to building deep and meaningful connections, are managed in an extraordinarily ineffective and inefficient way. The tools that technology provides are, for the majority of people, quite bulk, which is not very useful for the development of long term relationships. You can intensively use social media to develop your network, even with premium options. But still, we didn't find yet a way to hack the kind of connections that take time and effort to build, akin friendship.

Trust, as the main catalyzer of productive and durable relationships, is so difficult to hack. We may have even equations. [David Maister and Charles H. Green](#) did that when they split up trust into credibility, reliability, intimacy, and (in a negative way) self-orientation. But technological shortcuts are not developed yet, and this is something that might seem surprising in the era of big data and artificial intelligence.

Maybe we should create some [sous-vide](#) relationship building or a Slow Networking. Just like [the Slow Food](#) movement was to cuisine and the way we go to a restaurant.

27. How To Build Honest And Powerful Feedback

A lot of literature helps to give feedback, but knowing the person and building the things which need to be discussed should go first.

Many people give prefab feedback, which may be not only useless, but also frustrating, counterproductive, and a waste of time for both sides. As on many other occasions, feedback is sometimes considered more like an objective itself than a mere tool to reach a particular goal, namely, contribute to the growth and development of the other person.

I'm not an expert on feedback, I'm just an *aficionado* who has to give feedback lots of times, and who often ask for it. So I'm more on the practice side than on the theory one. You can find a thousand different articles from relevant sources (like this, this, or this, for example), or the good advice about the basics you can get in any session about the topic. Once I heard that you should always give feedback about what the other person DOES, not about what he or she IS, and I thought it was a great piece of advice, and a splendid technique to know what lines you should not cross. Of course, needless to say, that giving feedback doesn't have to be an excuse to spit out your truth or get something off your chest. It is not "blaming" or "complaining" time. It's not the time to push your strategy or gossip. Feedback is not a debrief, nor a way to convey orders for future actions on the chain of command. Feedback is not giving your opinion over a cup of coffee. Feedback is not an instrument to keep people alert, productive, and a bit afraid.

I know everyone knows, but let me just use this as a friendly reminder.

Feedback should be a way to convey an honest and deep attempt to help the other person to improve, to develop. In a word, to grow and be better. It's not an evaluation, it's not an appraisal. And objectively, there's something not working well about feedback, maybe because organizations have changed a lot during the latest decade or so. Gallup put it very clear:

We have found that *only 26% of employees strongly agree that the feedback they receive helps them do better work.* When most organizations had hierarchical, top-down, command-and-control structures as their primary decision-making method, the feedback was paramount. Information mostly needed to cascade downward in an organization, and the primary role of managers was to hold people accountable. Today, as leaders know, the workplace is radically different. Modern organizations are more decentralized, matrixed and agile. Employees have greater autonomy and are required to be creative in how work gets done. This means managers can't just give employees feedback about what they did "right" or "wrong." They must listen, ask questions, gain context, and create a two-way dialogue.

But let's go to the point. The trigger of my reflection was more about the kind of (crappy and bulky) feedback we are often asked to give, and how many of us understand this as normal behavior to follow. Allow me to put in positive terms: for me, feedback means addressing messages primarily intended to that person and no one else. I don't believe in "general feedback" whatsoever. Either you can touch the person as sincere as possible, making them face important spots of their reality to help them go over them and improve, or you simply get rid of your responsibility and pay lip service. It always has to be careful and respectful, based on facts, reasons, without sugarcoating but also removing any intention to do harm. Honest to the max, powerful to the max. You can summarize it in many formulas on how to give feedback (like this or this, for example).

Here's where I'd like to be of help with my humble experience. I can get hundreds of tips for the process of giving feedback, but not that many to know how to "read" the person and provide accurate insights to discover, emerge, or recognize things that are holding them back in some sense.

The following are some of the aspects I'm paying attention to when BUILDING my case to provide feedback to someone. After that, when you have things to say, the only thing you need is respect, some empathy, honest intention to help, and the will to go as deep as possible.

1. **Presence**: you cannot build good feedback if you don't pay attention to the personality of any individual. Here you can simplify it to Non-Verbal Communication, but it's a little bit deeper than that. It is about how does someone feels in a particular

moment, environment, or situation. It is about confidence, how do they use the espace, and expand in the room. Some might call it the vibe.

2. **Proactivity**: does that person wait for things to happen, or he/she goes for them? Does he/she have an objective or has an approach based on "let's see what's in it for me"?
3. ***"Radar" ability***: Is the person trying to figure out who you are, what are your interests? Is he working effectively in creating a connection or bond? Is he focused on "learning" you?
4. **Skills**: of course, traditional skills are essential. Best intentions die without proper skills, so you don't want to provide feedback about things the person is not still ready to achieve. The purpose is to help them grow, not to frustrate anyone.
5. **Interaction with other people**: basically, how does the person fit in a group, especially taking into account whether this aspect is providing a higher potential, or it is holding the person back.
6. **Ability to set the bar and go beyond expectations**: this is crucial for the process of growing and improvement, as it leads to what is considered to be excellence. It also shows the ability to read the context and know the benchmark, so the capacity to adapt.
7. **Strengths and weaknesses**: everyone is going to be confident about their strengths; we can go deep on that; but at the same time, we'll need to be careful when addressing something which might involve a flaw or weakness.

8. ***Gather tiny details*** and interest, use them to mirror, and build even more knowledge to keep learning about the person.
9. ***Is the whole profile coherent?*** When having a look at all the previous items together, is there anything that does not make sense? If so, try to understand why. This is also a fact check to know whether any part of your analysis is flawed or wrong in some way, and needs correction.
10. ***Finally, you need to imagine how is he/she going to deal with the ideas you have for the feedback.*** Is it going to cause any problem? Do you think it will be possible to have a relaxed (though maybe intense) and fruitful conversation about it? How is the feedback going to be handled? We should not say anything that would not be understood and accepted. It doesn't mean we should be unsubstantial, we simply should not bring up anything that cannot be handled positively.

With time, you get fluent in doing every step in much different order, without forgetting any significant aspect, or dismissing the ones that are not important (or redundant) in any specific case. You build your integrated picture almost subconsciously. And then, when you finally have that conversation, you realize where you were right or wrong, and also note it and learn for the next time, gaining your own experience out of it to make you better, too.

This could be a method or just a way to provoke a reflection about it. There's no more science here than experience, and a profound curiosity to truly learn about people and help them. Now that I think about it, that's probably the most critical part.

28. Build the Connectome of Your Business

Your identity may be explained by the map of connections between your neurons. And your network can define your organization.

Every day, an unquestionable reality becomes more evident: companies' structure is undergoing a profound transformation motivated by the penetration of technology to the last corner of its DNA.

Experts have widely commented on the need for the company to become a network company, flattening its structure and horizontalizing it, making it more flexible and interconnected.

From people's perspective, in whom most of the business knowledge is concentrated, new capacities are required. At the same time, they must be empowered as the main source and engine of value generation. In short, the company becomes an organization that, like everyone, is made up of a multitude of parties with entities that act as a network, fulfilling their function and responding to the organization's objectives and general strategy.

So far, nothing new, nothing unusual.

This, however, has paramount implications that may not yet have been fully understood. You probably heard of "connectome", an emerging concept in neuroscience developed by Professor Sebastian Seung from MIT. According to this theory, a person's consciousness, personality and character are strongly conditioned (to the point of explaining them) by their map of neural connections (the "connectome") rather than by their genetic information (their genome).

"I am more than my genes! What am I? I am my connectome." Such were the words of computational neuroscientist Sebastian Seung (Princeton Neuroscience Institute, Princeton, NJ, USA) in his TED Conference speech in 2010. He proposed that our connectome, the particular wiring of our brain, is what shapes our identity. Even though part of this neuronal map is programmed by our genes, Seung argued that neural activities—"encoding our thoughts, feelings, perceptions, and mental experiences"—can cause these connections to change, which makes each individual's connectome unique.

In general, this new branch of neuroscience, the "connectomics, "seeks to understand the brain from its map of nerve links, thus configuring a "fingerprint" that would identify each person. We have still a long way to go:

Yet the very scale of the problem is daunting. Only one connectome has been mapped to completion, and that was the roundworm, Caenorhabditis elegans. C. el- egans contains just 300 neurons joined by 7,000 connections, yet charting its neural connectivity took more than a decade to complete. "Your connectome is 100 bil- lion times larger [than C. elegans], with a million times more connections than your genome has letters," Seung writes.

The most important thing, in this case, is that, unlike the genome, the connectome is not invariable. Therefore each person could develop, evolve, from its most essential characteristics. This is especially so since our neurons can strengthen or weaken their synapses, even create new connections, depending on the events that occur to us.

And companies, like people, are increasingly defined by their relationships, by their connections, by their networking, both internally and externally. It is curious how professional and personal networks increasingly resemble a structure of brain connections, as shown, for example, by applications such as InMaps, through which each person can design the map of their relationships in the professional social network LinkedIn.

Our strength, our value, or that of our companies, is increasingly related to our connections. It is related to our map of links with other people or companies. They are part of us, and we are part of their organism in an interdependent, complex, unstable, changing way.

The individual loses relevance in favor of more complex, collective organisms that take on a life of their own. Our "connectome" changes day by day, but it defines and shapes our identity permanently. An identity that evolves very quickly, just like our environment. That is and will be the essential element of our reality: how we can build and manage our network and how we can continually modify it to adapt to the environment.

29. How To Build Long Term Value: Successful Mentorships

A conversation with <u>Vijay Ratthinam</u>, CEO of <u>PMI San Francisco Bay Area Chapter</u>, about his views on mentoring and future trends.

Project Management Institute (PMI) has more than 3,500 members in the Bay Area, and mentoring is one the passions of its CEO, Vijay Ratthinam, who has been leading the operations and hundreds of events during the latest years. Vijay's objective is to give back to the community, from his current senior position as a Program Manager at Salesforce, remembering that we all have encountered hardships and struggled during the initial stages of our professional career. Many people resort to coaching as a guide for professional development, but mentoring can be a more powerful and long-term solution.

A fruitful and lasting relationship with your mentor can be of much value for many aspects of your life. Even at a personal level, a mentor can turn to be a coach in certain elements, but also an advisor, a source for motivation. Above all, your mentor is interested in your success as much as you are. Mentoring is flexible; you can be mentored by a pear, a group, on even online. You should not limit to have only one mentor, but you may have different mentors according to diverse interests, objectives, and environments. The ultimate goal is helping people to navigate their careers, and your mentor can find the best way up when you feel stuck.

From Vijay and PMI's perspective, **one of the critical elements of a successful mentorship is measuring this relationship. We should** set up objectives and results to achieve, as it's no good if your mentor does not have a clue about what do you want, about the concrete targets you address. Success is something that may differ much for everyone, so we need to set it in clear terms: where do you want to be in six months, or one year. This will help you to get the right mentor, and it will be easier for him or her to help you. Every mentorship needs to have some time-bound and specific questions.

A second essential aspect of a successful mentorship would be related to something we forget many times. **The mentee is responsible for the relationship; he needs to remember he is in the driving seat**and being mindful of it at every moment. Without this, the relationship can go nice, but adrift.

A third aspect is a trust. Mentorship involves a lot of personal interrelations and sharing, so it becomes a combination of science and art. **We need the art to create trust, but we also need the science to track and define the metrics**, and needs. Once we do the mapping, we can find the areas we are doing well already and the ones that need improvement or fix something. In the end, the mentee and mentor have a cool project to work together. And the objective is that both are happy and successful.

The fourth principle we would like to highlight has to do with mentor profile: **the ideal mentor has a balance**

between knowledge and experience. Of course, a mentor never stops learning and getting trained, but the most relevant part of his value comes from his expertise and experiences.

And finally, the last principle relates to the common objectives of the mentees. **Often, mentees feel they cannot find a way to break through** or switch to the direction they want to go. They think their potential cannot be unleashed, and do not see a way to unlock it and achieve higher roles and responsibilities. In these situations, usually, the mentor has the key to a shift in the position. Vijay's message to the youngest is: "no matter what point of your career are you, look for a mentor, learn from him like reading a book which shows you a different world. It'll keep you from making many mistakes and will drive you in the right way".

30. Something's Changing On How Companies Deal With Employees

Airbnb's Talent Directory has become a hype in a couple of weeks, on its way to becoming a worldwide acknowledged best practice.

Last week I discovered a website called Airbnb's Talent Directory, and I thought it was an excellent idea. It is a neat, clean sheet with just a lot of cards, where you can find brief profiles of people who have worked at Airbnb. For most of them, there is a short description made by themselves, career and aspirations, and the main links to professional and personal social media. For many, there is also a link to a resume for a piece of more detailed knowledge and analysis. You can also browse and find information according to different filters, like forty-two cities in many countries, or next to forty functions to know the main focus of their job at Airbnb. You may also see if they are open to relocation or remote work.

Asking some friends in the HR business, they told me it is becoming a sort of best practice that went out of the covid situation. It seems quite simple, honest, and effective. When I discussed the initiative with some other friends at Airbnb, they openly say there's not any "not so bright" side in the project. Everything seemed positive (apart from, of course, the fact that the project's spark was a significant layoff of next to 2,000 workers due to covid situation). I tried to find and confront different opinions, to provide you with the pros and cons of the idea.

First, I found the version of the company, who actually published a short and effective note at Medium, through Dylan Hurd:

The past few months have been hard for all of us, but it has been inspiring to see everyone, especially the Airbnb community, support each other during an unprecedented time. Our CEO, Brian Chesky, recently announced the departure of nearly 1,900 employees. Among these employees are incredibly talented Engineers and Data Scientists who have contributed to Airbnb in uncountable ways.

To support our teammates departing Airbnb, we launched the Alumni Talent Directory, an opt-in directory which lists valued employees and contingent workers who have recently departed Airbnb. If you're currently hiring or looking for incredible talent, the Talent Directory is full of amazing Engineers and Data Scientists, among others.

I can't help to keep liking it. So I went to journalism, where we can always resort to negative perspectives and the dark side of any situation. What I found was, again, quite surprising.

Some were saying that Airbnb "shows the way to compassionate layoff." Ok, it's a way to put it, a bit emotional, but fair enough. It could resemble branded content, like "while announcing a global layoff, Airbnb did something unusual to allow its employees to leave with grace, and it is winning the hearts," as e27.com puts it. They are not the first, but they are definitely contributing to the creation of a new trend. And in a couple of weeks, hundreds of profiles are already in the directory.

Indeed, Airbnb was not the first to create and publish a talent directory. Down east, Singapore-based HOOQ published a similar directory to boost the chances of retrenched employees.
Another example came from a group of VC firms in Southeast Asia, which include Saison Capital, FutureLab, Jungle Ventures, and Alpha JWC Ventures.

Together they launched a 'community-led' initiative—known as SEAriously Awesome People List—Startup COVID-19 Layoffs—in March to help retrenched startup employees find new opportunities.

From another perspective, The Drum focused and reflected on whether "is there ever a good way to say goodbye?". By carrying out so simple (and extremely low cost) actions, "Airbnb has set a standard that many firms should look to. As he cut 25% of the workforce (1,900 from the firm's ranks of 7,500 employees), he gave a settlement amounted to around 14 weeks' pay plus a week's salary per year of employment. He also gave x, establishing an alumni placement team and talent directory, and allowing departing employees to keep their Apple laptops."

Best way to know they're going in the right direction or even creating some momentum? Some are following, like Uber, as "CEO Dara Khosrowshahi sent an email to employees Monday notifying them of the layoffs. Combined with previous reductions announced earlier this month, Uber will cut about 6,700 jobs or some 25% of its global workforce." But Uber decided to launch its own online directory for white-collar workers "to give our former colleagues the attention from recruiters they deserve," said Uber spokesperson Lois Van Der Laan. The Washington Post developed this kind of analysis during the latest weeks, too, depicting the practice as one more hype in Silicon Valley's techs. According to this Washington Post article, though, three former Airbnb employees impacted by the cuts, who spoke on the condition of anonymity, told The Post they were grateful to appear in the directory and have already received messages about its potential openings.

We know that outplacement has existed for decades, but it was the kind of process that market (and the involved workers) saw as a company paying for a conscience laundering. This looks different, as a smart and bold move in many senses, not only the most personal ones. It introduces the idea of community belonging beyond the company. You're not part of the community just while you have a contract, but you may be "one of ours" even though you need to go away. From another perspective, of course, Airbnb is building a reputation in moments when the public and the market is so sensitive that your action now might well become your future image. And finally, if things eventually get better, the company left open the door to many talented professionals, something which is really scarce (and therefore expensive) in the Bay Area and the Valley.

Real or crocodile tears; who cares; the page is up as a showroom of people who needs and deserve one new professional opportunity. What the heck, give them a round of applause.

31. You Will Never Come Back To The Office, And This Is A Really Smart Move

Major corporations are seriously thinking about turning remote work the default option for most of the employees.

A movement started. Twitter (and Square) told their employees they could continue working from home "forever." They are not the only ones. A month ago, Salesforce gave all employees the option to work from home for the rest of the year, regardless of when their local office location opens up. Zuckerberg predicts that "it's possible that over the next five to 10 years—maybe closer to 10 than five, but somewhere in that range—we could get to about half of the company working remotely permanently." Sundar Pichai, Google's CEO, told Google employees on Thursday to be ready to work remotely through October and possibly to the end of the year. A Google spokeswoman said most Google workers are expected to work from home until 2021.

And the list goes on and on. It's only a matter of time that the trend goes mainstream. This could be the most significant shift in productivity and profit for the last century. Internet and the Information Age can be a joke compared to this. The Industrial Revolution took people away from home. It urged them to believe that work was no longer at home or whereabouts. To be productive, they needed to go to a place (a factory) where owners organized the work to make the most of every penny. And we've been swallowing that for generations, more than two centuries. In the 20th century, a new variable appeared, and transport made commute an annoying extension of our working day. When car use growth was faster than road development or capacity, commute double or tripled in certain areas. Shortening commute would mean paying a fortune for a tiny apartment, and a pressure to get salaries higher to pay insane housing bills. This was the story in most metropolitan areas. Result? Nine to five could become seven to seven. If you add up environmental costs, congestion, and problems with urban mobility, how we get so far seems impossible.

ZDNet explored it in detail:

It's not just the office managers who've warmed up to people working from home. A Glassdoor survey showed "67% of employees would support the decision by their employer to mandate employees 'work from home indefinitely.'"
Generally speaking younger workers are more confident about this than their older counterparts, "68% of employees aged 18–34 reported being confident in doing their work remotely if they have to, compared to 44% of employees aged 55–64." Interestingly, "71% of employed parents with children under age 18 said that they feel confident they can efficiently do their job remotely."
IT management is also OK with this new work from home model. An IDG survey found 71% say the coronavirus

pandemic "has created a more positive view of remote workplaces." This is already making them look at "how they plan for office space, tech staffing and overall staffing in the future."

But this seems about to break such a long term trend. We may be facing the most critical outsourcing process of modern history. We're moving workers back home for the first time since 1900, making them happy, productive, less poor, and passing them the cost of their extremely expensive workplace. BYOD will appear to have been the seed for PYOO. In the New Normal, Provide Your Own Office would finally be mainstream.

If you think about it, it's sad that no one had the guts to be bold enough to do it before. It couldn't have been any other way; human nature is fearful and tends to remain in the comfort zone. But now that everybody saw that everything's ok (unmasking managers who were dying to show the crowd had to be micromanaged), it's time for the big move. The experiment proved to be more successful than ever imagined. Over the last few weeks, we've seen reports that major corporations. JPMorgan, Facebook, Capital One, Amazon, Microsoft, Zillow, and others, announced that they're extending their work-from-home policies. Unstoppable.

Forbes already saw it very clear a few weeks ago.

Chief financial officers recognize the **enormous potential savings they'd realize by not needing to house thousands of workers** in highly expensive skyscrapers in overcrowded cities. A thousand square feet in the best building of major cities can be easily over 100k a year. You can do the math.

Human resources professionals know that permitting people to work from home offers their employees a **better quality and balance of work and life**.

Companies will no longer look for job seekers within their immediate geographical region. Job seekers now won't be restricted to work within the confines of their geographic boundaries.

It's like a vast, really globalized marketplace. The labor market might easily be called Upwork. You know what? I got a job in New York, but I prefer to live in Berlin. How challenging would this be for regulations?

Besides, major corporations can show their commitment and environmental concerns, a new era of Corporate Social Responsibility, Shared Value, call it whatever you like. And the best part is that it could even be finally true.

Finally, the world of Digital (work) By Default is arriving. And guess what? It can be a win-win-win-win-win. For companies, for workers, for society, for governments, and the planet. Would it be possible that the philosopher's stone was just under our nose, and we did not realize it?

We know that many companies, many workers, many countries, many governments, are not ready. The whole system can have limits for retail, transport, manufacturing, agriculture, hospitality, but it should create jobs. Let's promote a radical change in real estate. Blue-collar and white-collar? Why not a new group of digital-collars?

Isn't it worth giving it a try?

32. The Basics of a High Quality Networking

Your relationships must be crafted, not bulk. Thousands of business cards won't bring you business.

An old proverb says that we have two ears and a mouth to listen to double what we speak. We all felt that the person in front of you is merely waiting for you to stop talking. The point is that listening carefully, as simple as it seems, is the key to understanding, analyzing, and communicating. When we think about communication, we think more about "sending" well than about "receiving" correctly; and that is a mistake.

I recently met a colleague whom I had not seen for a long time. I was happy about that unexpected meeting in a remote place in Europe, and we chatted about new trends in business and professional relationships.

"Forget about it," he said, "networking is for the evenings, but does not close deals. The next morning, it is a fact that in most cases, that conversation with your friendly table partner will not happen to grow, and that you may not even have time to send an email to the people you spoke to." I thought he was just kidding, that we were having one more of those hollow conversations. But as he is a person I respect a lot, with a long experience in the business world, I hesitated and promised to reflect on it calmly later.

And indeed, I think he was partly right. We have more powerful tools to access more contacts, more extensive networks. And precisely for this reason, we must continue to take great care of people, prioritize quality over quantity, and establish clear objectives both in what we seek and in what we can offer and hope to obtain from these (new) relationships.

The temptation to forever expand our network, sometimes with no much sense, does not significantly improve our company's results. It's maybe the opposite. Possibly it takes time that we'd need to do what is really beneficial: working and taking care of the details of the relationship with those with whom we have established a positive, personal and productive trust connection. In short: take care of our valuable relationships beyond when we need to ask them for something.

I think my colleague wanted to say that he was getting more and more tired of wasting time on endless dinners, which apparently favor business relationships, but which are really only a relic of old-fashioned ways of doing things. Maybe he's right, or perhaps it's just that he's been bored in recent events. But I was delighted to see him; I have to call him because we came up with a couple of exciting ideas that could go well.

Do you believe in coincidences? Neither do I. Since I had that conversation with my friend, I received emails and calls from people of whom I had not known anything for months. Even from some people that I still know little about, and who have proposed to meet and explore possible collaborations in different projects. Besides, some other companies asked for our contribution to inspiring projects. The result is that over the following few weeks, we had a really interesting "true" networking, face-to-face, personal, and best quality on the agenda, no flat Facetime.

That reminded me of an article that hit my screen some time ago, written by Dorie Clark on Forbes. She reflected precisely on networking techniques with your professional networks, which she illustrated through the example of Michael Katz, a marketing consultant who published several books and produced a newsletter every two weeks with more than 7,500 subscribers in 40 countries. Hoping to find innovative keys, what I really saw was groundbreaking back to basics. You know, the difference between old and classic is a matter of letting time goes by.

The article title said it all: "Newsletters, Emails And Coffee Dates: Win Business By Going Old-School." The conversation between Dorie Clark and Michael Katz leaves us some gems that we all know: "I've been waiting for newsletters to stop working for about ten years since they stopped being the latest thing, but it didn't happen"; "Facts and information are good, but there's no shortage of that," he says. "From the outside looking in, all financial planners, consultants, coaches, recruiters, doctors, whatever, seem equally qualified. The differentiating factor is the person or persons who write the newsletter. Tell stories, speak like a human being, connect." Simple, huh? Complicated, right?

Let me use some irony; it does not stop here: "Building a high public profile or social media following is great, but new business is most likely to come from people you know. By focusing on our existing contacts primarily, we're gaming the system." Wow.

And finally, it focuses your odds of success in two completely revolutionary elements (really?): That people think that you are very good at what you do and that you are an authentic, real person ("likable" was their word).

When you have the truth in your face and don't notice, it hurts. Shall the man be right?

33. Fear Is The Worst Enemy For Teams

Remove fear from your teams, or help them to manage uncertainty. That could be the only way to keep trust as the most critical asset for your organization.

I like a lot a Simon Sinek's definition for leadership: "The real work of a leader is not being in charge; it's about taking care of those in our charge". We could add that your job as a leader is to create the conditions so that your team can perform their tasks as smooth as possible. You make life easier for them to do their best, and to achieve the best results for the whole organization.

You work hard to put everyone at their top of the potential and bring them to places they not even knew or believed they could reach. You make them grow; that's what a leader does. And therefore, leadership is not something you can put on your agenda as one more 'to do'. Oh, I didn't do much leadership this week because I had a bunch of other urgent matters.

No. Leadership is a full-time job that we need to put to an unconscious competence level, the highest of four stages. Zainab Zaki explains quick and well in a Medium article:

Unconscious Competence—The final stage where we've mastered the new skill or behavior such that its instinctual. We aren't practicing anymore. While we're still learning and growing, we've established a strong foundation and can be confident about our competency in that area.

That's what a leader can do, what needs to learn how to do. And leadership is a skill that can be taught, can be practiced, and can be trained like a muscle.

As Sinek continues, we're trained to have the competences to do our job, and then, when we become so good at doing it, we can be promoted to be responsible for people that now do the things we used to do. Usually, we're not trained to be responsible for the team, and what do we do? Of course, micromanage. And we become managers, not leaders, mostly because we don't know how to help them do "our" old job. You're no longer responsible for the job but responsible for the people who are doing the job.

And then we have that awful feeling that "we're not working anymore," but solving all day other problems that "stop us from our doing our work." And we feel confused, useless. And thus, so do our teams. They need you strong; they need you to tell them everything's going to be ok during your watch. You need to give them all the credit and take on your shoulders all the stress and responsibility. The manager points out what you did wrong; the leader would ask if you need any help to do your job better. Leadership creates trust and the most comfortable environment for the people to give their best.

How does science approach this? When your organization is very demanding, but not caring about people, maybe they can get results. But still, they will not reach their potential, not in terms of personal development and teams or in terms of the whole organization.

From an excellent worker to a growing leader, this transition is one that many do not understand or are not able to do. Sometimes it happens to entrepreneurs who think that by being the best engineer, they'll be the best CEO for the new company. Sometimes it occurs to those skilled workers becoming executives: they simply don't know that their only job from then on is to take care of people. To make them happy, to get them productive, in order to make customers happy. Don't serve your client; serve your people, and they will make the client happy.

I know you've heard it many times. But I'm sorry, it's what works in the long run. Or, at least, it is the way you should want your organization to work in the long term.

In stressful situations, like the one we're going through these days, fear and uncertainty can break the balance. You may think what you need in this kind of environment is resilient, strong people to take care of themselves. That might be true, and it would save much work on your side. But even the strongest will need your help as a leader to navigate tough times.

Be ready and alert because uncertainty and fear can break trust, break bonds, and the balance of your organization. And as it is quite unlikely that fear breaks skills, it might well break trust by sky-rocketing self-orientation and self-interest. A selfish team is not a team anymore.

As Charles H. Green puts it in his Trust Equation, fear and uncertainty can be very dangerous for the balance of your team, as it can boost self-orientation and dramatically reduce intimacy, and even reliability. And building on trust is your most crucial foundation as a leader

The current extremely VUCA times is putting teams into much stress. You know the old saying: give someone a lot of money, and you'll discover their true nature. Put someone under fear and uncertainty, and you'll also find out who they are. Your job as a leader is keeping them safe and happy. And above all, in hard times, as the song was saying: "You could save me from the way I tend to be."

CONCLUSION: Take control, you're in the driving seat

It's a sheer contradiction: in times of volatility, uncertainty, and permanent change, we want to take control.

But this is strategy: travel to the future, see all the options and work hard to make your preferred one happen.

So many authors talked about the future; we can find thousands of wise thoughts. Let me just share a few of them to insist on the idea that we should be ready to go forward being in the driving seat. It's not easy, but at least you'll know where you want to go.

"If you don't think about the future, you cannot have one." John Golsworthy.

"The future is not something we enter. The future is something we create." Leonard I. Sweet.

"The best way to predict the future is to create it." Peter Drucker.
"The future belongs to those who prepare for it today." Malcolm X.

"Prediction is very difficult, especially if it's about the future." Niels Bohr.

"The future has a way of arriving unannounced." George Will.

"The future rewards those who press on." Barack Obama.

"Control your own destiny or someone else will." Jack Welch.

"Destiny is no matter of chance. It is a matter of choice. It is not a thing to be waited for, it is a thing to be achieved." William Jennings Bryan.

"Luck can be assisted. It is not all chance with the wise." Baltasar Gracian.

www.ingramcontent.com/pod-product-compliance
Lightning Source LLC
Chambersburg PA
CBHW031628210526
45464CB00004B/1798